SUPER SCIENCE Investigations

Table of Contents

Life Science

Earth Science

Physical Science

Data Collection Sheets

About This Book

Children's insatiable curiosity makes them much like scientists. Children love to investigate unfamiliar things and then analyze what they've discovered. *Super Science Investigations* builds upon this natural curiosity by structuring simple investigations that help children think scientifically as well as become better problem solvers. This collection of 30 easy-to-implement, hands-on science investigations is divided into ten life science case files, ten earth science case files, and ten physical science case files. Each investigation case file contains one student-centered investigation that begins with a question for the students to answer, such as "Why Are My Thumbs Important?" The case file also contains everything you need to guide students through successfully completing the investigation:

- the purpose of the investigation
- a complete materials list
- background information
- suggestions for how to introduce the investigation to students
- step-by-step instructions for completing the investigation
- a handy "Case File Conclusion" section providing an explanation of possible outcomes to the investigation
- optional questions for further investigation
- a reproducible data collection sheet or pattern

How to Use This Book

Because a teacher's time is so valuable, each super science investigation is designed with simplicity, flexibility, and ease in mind. The book is divided into three sections: life science, earth science, and physical science. A handy skills grid is provided on page 4 to help you quickly and easily determine the specific skill(s) addressed in each investigation. Once you've selected the appropriate investigation, carefully read over each section of the selected case file (see the sample investigation on page 3). Each two-page investigation case file contains all the information you need to successfully complete the investigation with your students.

A student reproducible accompanies each investigation. The reproducibles are data collection sheets designed for students to use during the investigation. All the reproducible pages are labeled with the appropriate section name and case number and are located at the back of the book (pages 66–95). Page 96 is a blank data collection sheet that can be programmed to meet the specific needs of your students.

The investigations are designed as small-group or whole-class activities. However, most can be altered to adapt to the specific needs of your classroom. Each activity concludes with a list of questions for further investigation. Although optional, these thought-provoking questions will come in handy when students want to further investigate a topic.

Sample Investigation Case File

The case file stamp identifies the section name (life, earth, or physical science) and the investigation case number.

The question for students to investigate is located here.

"The Investigation" provides step-by-step instructions for guiding students through the investigation.

"Purpose" informs the teacher of the science skill(s) covered in the investigation. "Materials" alerts the teacher to any materials needed for the investigation.

"Further Investigation" provides related questions for students to discuss and/or investigate after completing the main investigation. (This is optional.)

"Background for the Teacher" provides important facts related to the investigation.

"Getting Started" details any advance preparations as well as how to introduce students to the investigation.

"Case File Conclusion" provides an explanation of possible outcomes to the investigation.

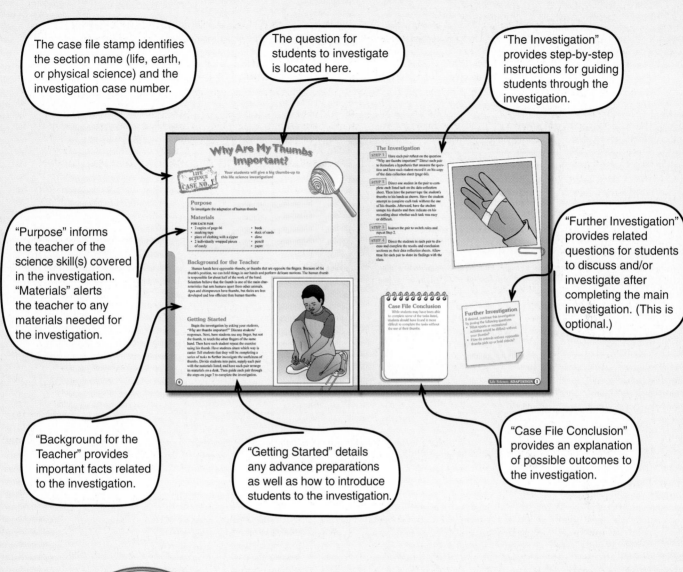

A student data collection sheet is used during the investigation.

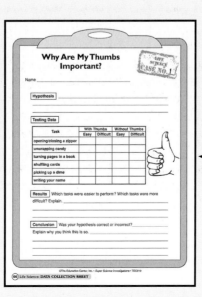

Life Science Skills	Case 1	Case 2	Case 3	Case 4	Case 5	Case 6	Case 7	Case 8	Case 9	Case 10
To investigate the adaptation of human thumbs	●									
To discover how an animal adapts to its habitat		●								
To investigate how adaptations in an animal's body structure enhance the chances of survival for the species			●							
To classify living things				●						
To observe how flowers depend on bees for pollination					●					
To identify the major parts of plant cells						●				
To understand how short-term memory works							●			
To understand bile's role in the digestion of food								●		
To understand and measure lung vital capacity									●	
To examine how exercise and rest affect heart rate										●

Earth Science Skills	Case 1	Case 2	Case 3	Case 4	Case 5	Case 6	Case 7	Case 8	Case 9	Case 10
To observe how the texture of a soil affects how much water it can hold	●									
To model how the earth's surface changes as a result of erosion by water		●								
To observe and describe the physical differences between sand and potting soil			●							
To identify possible man-made and natural sources of airborne pollution at school				●						
To gain understanding of how much recyclable trash one classroom generates weekly					●					
To observe how the water cycle works						●				
To construct and use instruments to measure wind direction and wind speed							●			
To understand the sun's position in relation to the earth								●		
To understand that the earth's rotation causes stars to appear to move across the sky									●	
To compare the relative sizes of the planets in relation to Earth										●

Physical Science Skills	Case 1	Case 2	Case 3	Case 4	Case 5	Case 6	Case 7	Case 8	Case 9	Case 10
To determine whether matter can be invisible	●									
To discover a common material that exists in all three states of matter		●								
To understand the difference between mixtures and compounds			●							
To observe and describe how matter changes when it is heated				●						
To observe whether air or a solid material is a better conductor of sound					●					
To observe how light bends as it passes through an object						●				
To observe the effects of opposite forces acting on an object							●			
To observe how various modifications can affect the flight of paper airplanes								●		
To understand that electrical circuits require a complete path through which a current can pass									●	
To identify the characteristics of good conductors										●

SUPER SCIENCE
Investigations

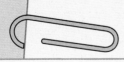

Managing Editors: Karen A. Brudnak, Cindy Mondello
Editor at Large: Diane Badden
Staff Editors: Lauren E. Cox, Sherry McGregor
Contributing Writers: Michelle Bauml, Shawna Graham, Liz Harrell, Terry Healy, Kim A. Howe, Starin Lewis, Laura Wagner
Copy Editors: Tazmen Carlisle, Amy Kirtley-Hill, Kristy Parton, Debbie Shoffner, Cathy Edwards Simrell
Art Coordinator: Greg D. Rieves
Artists: Pam Crane, Chris Curry, Shane Freeman, Theresa Lewis Goode, Clevell Harris, Ivy L. Koonce, Clint Moore, Greg D. Rieves, Rebecca Saunders, Barry Slate, Stuart Smith, Donna K. Teal
The Mailbox® Books.com: Judy P. Wyndham (MANAGER); Jennifer Tipton Bennett (DESIGNER/ARTIST); Karen White (INTERNET COORDINATOR); Paul Fleetwood, Xiaoyun Wu (SYSTEMS)

President, The Mailbox Book Company™: Joseph C. Bucci
Director of Book Planning and Development: Chris Poindexter
Curriculum Director: Karen P. Shelton
Book Development Managers: Cayce Guiliano, Elizabeth H. Lindsay, Thad McLaurin
Editorial Planning: Kimberley Bruck (DIRECTOR); Debra Liverman, Sharon Murphy, Susan Walker (TEAM LEADERS)
Editorial and Freelance Management: Karen A. Brudnak; Sarah Hamblet, Hope Rodgers (EDITORIAL ASSISTANTS)
Editorial Production: Lisa K. Pitts (TRAFFIC MANAGER); Lynette Dickerson (TYPE SYSTEMS); Mark Rainey (TYPESETTER)
Librarian: Dorothy C. McKinney

©2004 by THE EDUCATION CENTER, INC.
All rights reserved.
ISBN# 1-56234-593-1

Why Are My Thumbs Important?

LIFE SCIENCE CASE NO. 1

Your students will give a big thumbs-up to this life science investigation!

Purpose

To investigate the adaptation of human thumbs

Materials

FOR EACH PAIR

- 2 copies of page 66
- masking tape
- piece of clothing with a zipper
- 2 individually wrapped pieces of candy
- book
- deck of cards
- dime
- pencil
- paper

Background for the Teacher

Human hands have *opposable thumbs,* or thumbs that are opposite the fingers. Because of the thumb's position, we can hold things in our hands and perform delicate motions. The human thumb is responsible for about half of the work of the hand. Scientists believe that the thumb is one of the main characteristics that sets humans apart from other animals. Apes and chimpanzees have thumbs, but theirs are less developed and less efficient than human thumbs.

Getting Started

Begin the investigation by asking your students, "Why are thumbs important?" Discuss students' responses. Next, have students use any finger, but not the thumb, to touch the other fingers of the same hand. Then have each student repeat the exercise using his thumb. Have students share which way is easier. Tell students that they will be completing a series of tasks to further investigate the usefulness of thumbs. Divide students into pairs, supply each pair with the materials listed, and have each pair arrange its materials on a desk. Then guide each pair through the steps on page 7 to complete the investigation.

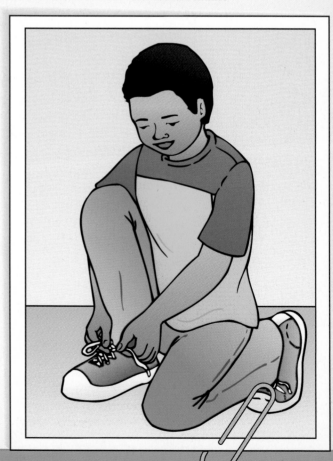

The Investigation

STEP 1 Have each pair reflect on the question "Why are thumbs important?" Direct each pair to formulate a hypothesis that answers the question and have each student record it on his copy of the data collection sheet (page 66).

STEP 2 Direct one student in the pair to complete each listed task on the data collection sheet. Then have the partner tape the student's thumbs to his hands as shown. Have the student attempt to complete each task without the use of his thumbs. Afterward, have the student untape his thumbs and then indicate on his recording sheet whether each task was easy or difficult.

STEP 3 Instruct the pair to switch roles and repeat Step 2.

STEP 4 Direct the students in each pair to discuss and complete the results and conclusion sections on their data collection sheets. Allow time for each pair to share its findings with the class.

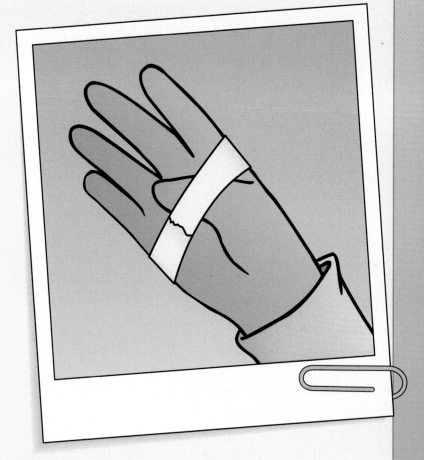

Case File Conclusion

While students may have been able to complete some of the tasks listed, students should have found it more difficult to complete the tasks without the use of their thumbs.

Further Investigation

If desired, continue this investigation by posing the following questions:

- What sports or recreational activities would be difficult without your thumbs?
- How do animals without opposable thumbs pick up or hold objects?

How Can a Polar Bear Survive in the Arctic?

LIFE SCIENCE CASE NO. 2

Brrr! Intrigue your students with this icy investigation of how animals survive in the bitter Arctic cold.

Purpose

To discover how an animal adapts to its habitat

Materials

FOR EACH PAIR
- copy of page 67
- 8 latex gloves
- Crisco shortening
- plastic knife
- bowl of ice water

Background for the Teacher

For plants and animals, being able to adapt to their environment is an important key to survival. An *adaptation* is any characteristic of an organism that helps it survive and reproduce in its environment. Organisms produce more offspring than can survive, and those that have better adapted to their environments are more likely to survive and reproduce.

Getting Started

Begin the activity by defining the term *adaptation* and then asking your students, "What are some adaptations that help animals survive?" Discuss their responses. Then tell your students that they are going to investigate how polar bears survive in the icy temperatures of the Arctic. Divide students into pairs and then give each pair the materials listed above. Guide the pairs through the steps on page 9 to complete the investigation.

The Investigation

STEP 1 Instruct each pair to reflect on the question "How can a polar bear survive in the Arctic?" Have each pair formulate a hypothesis that answers the question and record it on the data collection sheet (page 67).

STEP 2 Have a student from each pair put on a pair of latex gloves. Next, direct the student's partner to use the plastic knife to coat one glove with a ¼-inch layer of Crisco shortening. Then have the partner carefully assist the student in putting on a second glove over the shortening-coated glove and a second glove over the uncoated glove.

STEP 3 On your signal, have the student place both gloved hands into the bowl of ice water. Ask the student to describe what she feels. Instruct the student's partner to record her responses on the data collection sheet. Have the student carefully remove and dispose of the gloves.

STEP 4 Next, have the other student in the pair complete Steps 2–3. Then direct the pair to discuss and complete the results and conclusion sections on the data collection sheet. Set aside time for each pair to share its findings.

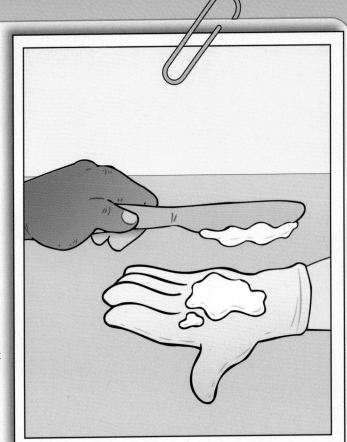

Case File Conclusion

The students will most likely find that the hand inside the shortening-coated glove doesn't feel as cold as the hand in the other glove. A polar bear survives in the Arctic because it has a layer of fat, or blubber. Like the Crisco shortening, the blubber acts as an insulator to keep the animal warm.

Further Investigation

If desired, continue this investigation by posing the following questions:
- How would a thinner or thicker coating of Crisco shortening affect the experiment?
- What other adaptations help a polar bear survive in the Arctic?
- What other animals have adapted to the Arctic cold?

If a Penguin Has Wings, Why Can't It Fly?

LIFE SCIENCE CASE NO. 3

Your students will love this cool experiment about animal adaptations!

Purpose

To investigate how adaptations in an animal's body structure enhance the chances of survival for the species

Materials

FOR THE TEACHER
- oaktag
- 4 copies of wing pattern (Figure 1)

FOR EACH PAIR
- copy of page 68
- access to wing templates in different sizes
- scissors
- white paper
- 4 cotton balls
- tape

Background for the Teacher

Birds are the only animals that have feathers. Feathers help birds stay warm and dry and help them fly. Although all birds have wings and feathers, not all birds fly. Some run, walk, or swim. These birds use their wings for balance or as flippers. Over time, these birds have *adapted* to their environments, adjusting to survive in the conditions in which they live.

Millions of years ago, penguins were able to fly. But because they spent so much time in the water, their wings began to change. Today their wings look like flippers and are used to help the penguin move through the water. As a result, penguins can swim about 20 miles an hour underwater but cannot fly.

Getting Started

In advance, make four copies of the wing pattern (Figure 1) and cut as indicated to make four different-size wings. Trace the wings onto oaktag, making enough templates so that pairs of students will have access to each size. Label the templates with the wing size.

Begin the activity by asking your students to name the characteristics of birds. Discuss students' responses. Then ask students if a penguin is a bird. Continue by asking students the question, "If a penguin has wings, why can't it fly?" Have students share their ideas. Then tell students they are going to conduct an investigation to discover why penguins can't fly. Pair students; then guide the pairs through the steps on page 11 to complete the investigation.

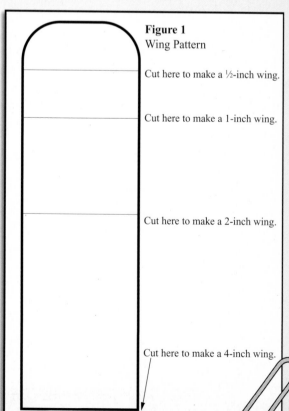

Figure 1
Wing Pattern

Cut here to make a ½-inch wing.

Cut here to make a 1-inch wing.

Cut here to make a 2-inch wing.

Cut here to make a 4-inch wing.

The Investigation

STEP 1 Have student pairs reflect on the question "If a penguin has wings, why can't it fly?" Direct each pair to formulate a hypothesis that answers the question and record it on the data collection sheet (page 68).

STEP 2 Have each pair use the oaktag wing templates to trace on white paper two wings in each of the four sizes and then cut them out.

STEP 3 Explain that each cotton ball represents the body of a penguin. Instruct the pair to tape a set of matching wings to each penguin.

STEP 4 Direct one student in each pair to hold a penguin at a specified height with its wings horizontal to the ground. Then instruct the student to drop it. Have the other student count the number of seconds it takes for the penguin to reach the floor and then note the time on the data collection sheet. Instruct each pair to repeat the process with the remaining penguins. Remind them to drop each penguin from the same height and to count each flight the same way.

STEP 5 Have each pair discuss and complete the results and conclusion sections on the data collection sheet. Set aside time for students to share their findings with the class.

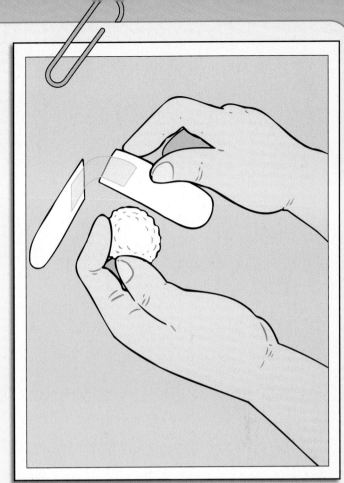

Case File Conclusion

Students most likely discovered that the penguin with the longest set of wings stayed in the air the longest amount of time, and the one with the shortest set of wings stayed in the air the shortest amount of time. The shortest set of wings represents a penguin's wings.

Further Investigation

If desired, continue this investigation by posing the following questions:

- How might a penguin adapt if the water temperature began to rise?
- How have penguins' feet adapted due to the time they spend in the water?

How Can Living Things Be Classified?

LIFE SCIENCE CASE NO. 4

Help students sort out classification with this fun investigative activity!

Purpose
To classify living things

Materials
FOR EACH PAIR
- copy of page 69
- small cup of mixed dried beans
- glue

Background for the Teacher

Scientists classify all living things into large groups called *kingdoms.* There are five kingdoms: animals, plants, fungi, protists (such as amoebas), and monerans (such as bacteria). The living things within a kingdom share characteristics that make them different from the living things in other kingdoms. Scientists subdivide the kingdoms into other groups, including *phyla* or *divisions, classes, orders, families, genera, species,* and *varieties* or *subspecies.* The more a group is subdivided, the greater the similarity among its members.

Getting Started

In advance, divide several bags of dried mixed beans into separate cups (enough for one cup per every two students). To begin the activity, ask students to get out their backpacks. Have them name characteristics that make their backpacks different. Have students gather a variety of backpacks and sort them by a specified *attribute* (a characteristic or quality), such as color. After the backpacks are sorted by color, call out another attribute, such as number of pockets or number of zippers and have students further subdivide their groups. After several examples, have students return to their seats. Then explain to your students that just as they divided and subdivided their backpacks based on attributes, scientists divide and subdivide living things based on different criteria such as common attributes. Further explain that the class is going to investigate how living things can be classified.

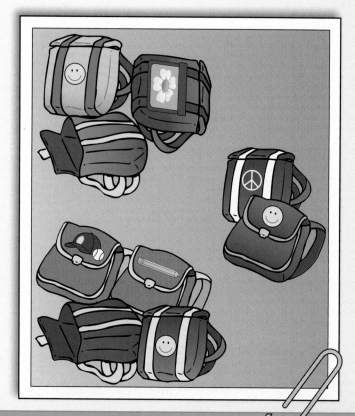

The Investigation

STEP 1 Instruct each pair to reflect on the question "How can living things be classified?" Direct each pair to formulate a hypothesis that answers the question. Direct one student in each pair to record the hypothesis on the data collection sheet (page 69).

STEP 2 Direct each pair to pour the beans from the cup. Then explain that each dried bean represents a newly discovered plant. Have pairs examine the plants carefully.

STEP 3 Direct each pair to sort the plants into different groups, each based on different criteria, such as a physical attribute.

STEP 4 Instruct the pair to glue one plant from each group onto a different box in the testing data section of the data collection sheet. Have the pair give the group a name and write the name beneath the plant, along with a brief description of the plants in the group and the criteria used to classify the plants.

STEP 5 Have each pair discuss and complete the results and conclusion sections of the data collection sheet. Set aside time for each pair to share its classifications and descriptions.

Case File Conclusion

Students will likely discover that their categories are based on easily identifiable physical attributes, such as size, shape, and color.

Further Investigation

If desired, continue this investigation by posing the following questions:
- Can the groups be further subdivided?
- Can living things be classified by criteria other than physical attributes?

How Do Flowers and Bees Work Together?

LIFE SCIENCE CASÉ NÓ. 5

This honey of an experiment investigates the interdependence of animals and plants.

Purpose

To observe how flowers depend on bees for pollination

Materials

FOR EACH STUDENT
• copy of page 70

FOR EACH GROUP
• permanent marker
• 3 plastic cups
• 10–12 cotton balls
• 3 different flavors of powdered fruit drink
• 3 cotton swabs
• small cup of water

Background for the Teacher

Plants and animals help each other. Plants provide animals with food and shelter. Animals help plants by moving plant seeds to new places or by aiding plants in making seeds. Flowers and bees provide one example of how plants and animals help each other. A flower provides a bee with pollen and nectar. The bee eats the pollen and later uses the nectar to make honey. As the bee crawls around on the flower, pollen grains stick to the bee. When the bee lands on another flower, some of this pollen brushes off, starting the flower's fertilization process. More flowers are pollinated by bees than by any other insect.

Getting Started

Begin the investigation by explaining to students that plants and animals need each other. Share a few examples, such as a squirrel moving seeds (nuts) from one place to another and a bird making its nest out of plant materials. Then ask, "How do flowers and bees work together?" Discuss students' responses. Then tell students they are going to conduct an investigation to test their responses. Divide students into groups of three and distribute the listed materials. Then guide each group through the steps on page 15 to complete the investigation.

The Investigation

STEP 1 Ask each student to think about the question "How do flowers and bees work together?" Direct him to formulate a hypothesis that answers the question and to record it on his data collection sheet (page 70).

STEP 2 Have each group use the marker to label its cups "A," "B," and "C." Direct the group to place a few cotton balls in the bottom of each cup and then sprinkle a different flavor of powdered drink mix in each. Explain to students that each cup represents a flower and the drink mix is the pollen.

STEP 3 Have each student wet the end of a cotton swab, tap off any excess, and then dip it into one of the labeled cups. Explain that the cotton swab represents a bee landing on a flower. Have each student record his observations on his data collection sheet. Next, have each student dip the same swab in the other two cups and record what he sees.

STEP 4 Have the group discuss its results. Instruct each student to complete the results and conclusion sections on his data collection sheet. Allow time to discuss the results as a class.

Case File Conclusion

Students will likely see that the cotton balls in each cup have more than one color on them, demonstrating how pollination occurs. Something similar happens when a bee lands on a flower. The bee moves around, gathering nectar. During this time, it becomes dusted with pollen. The pollen is then transported to the next flower the bee visits.

Further Investigation

If desired, continue this investigation by posing the following questions:
- How do flowers attract bees?
- What are other ways animals help plants?
- What factors might affect pollination?

What Is Inside a Plant Cell?

LIFE SCIENCE CASE NO. 6

Help your students focus on the structures of plant cells with this life science investigation.

Purpose

To identify the major parts of plant cells

Materials

FOR EACH STUDENT
- copy of page 71

FOR EACH GROUP
- onion section, sliced vertically
- tweezers
- microscope slide
- eyedropper
- microscope
- water
- coverslip

Background for the Teacher

A cell is the basic unit in all living things. Some life-forms consist of just a single cell, and others consist of many cells. For example, the human body is made up of over ten trillion cells.

Each cell's structure and contents allow it to do a specialized job that helps keep the organism alive. All cells have membranes around them that control what enters and leaves. Plant cells also have cell walls, which make the cells' shapes rigid. The activities of most cells are controlled by the nucleus. Cytoplasm is the substance between a cell's membrane and its nucleus. The vacuoles, spaces in the cytoplasm, are where the cell's food and chemicals are stored. Photosynthesis takes place in chloroplasts found in the cytoplasm in plant cells.

Getting Started

Begin the investigation by asking your students to name the smallest and the largest living things they can think of. Discuss their responses and review with students that all living things, from the smallest to the largest, are made up of cells. Ask students to reflect on the question "What is inside a plant cell?" Then divide students into groups. Explain that each group will examine plant cells with a microscope to find out what is inside a cell. Then guide each group through the steps on page 17 to complete the investigation.

The Investigation

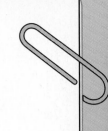

STEP 1 Direct each group to formulate a hypothesis that answers the question "What is inside a plant cell?" and have each student record it on her data collection sheet (page 71).

STEP 2 Explain to students that each plant cell includes a cell wall, a cell membrane, and a nucleus, plus vacuoles and chloroplasts inside its cytoplasm. Discuss these terms. Then explain that each group will use a microscope to find the parts of an onion skin cell. Instruct each group to follow the steps shown in Figure 1 to prepare its onion skin slide.

STEP 3 Show each group how to use the microscope to study the onion skin's cells. Next, have each student in the group find an onion skin cell and draw what she sees on her data collection sheet. Then guide the students to identify and label the cell wall, membrane, nucleus, and cytoplasm.

STEP 4 Direct the students in each group to discuss and complete the results and conclusion sections on their data collection sheets. Set aside time for each group to share its findings with the class.

Case File Conclusion

Students should find that the onion skin's cell walls, membranes, and cytoplasm are easy to see. Identifying a cell's nucleus, chloroplasts, and vacuoles inside the cytoplasm may be more difficult, but students should understand that the cytoplasm contains other cell parts.

Figure 1

1. Fold the top of the onion section until you see a thin layer of skin. Use the tweezers to peel this layer away from the onion.

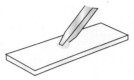

2. Place the skin in the center of the slide.

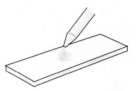

3. Use the eyedropper to cover the onion skin layer with a drop of water.

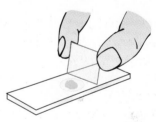

4. Carefully place the coverslip over the water drop.

Further Investigation

If desired, continue this investigation by posing the following questions:
- Are the cells of different kinds of plants the same or different?
- How many cell parts can you find in prepared slides of animal tissue?
- How are animal and plant cells different?

Why Can I Remember Some Things but Not Others?

Your students won't forget this investigation of short-term memory!

Purpose

To understand how short-term memory works

Materials

FOR THE TEACHER
- bag containing 15 different items (such as a paper clip, scissors, pencil, ruler, rock, feather, penny, and comb)

FOR EACH STUDENT
- copy of page 72

Background for the Teacher

Memory is the ability to recall something that a person has learned or experienced. If the brain had no memory, no learning could take place. Each situation would be brand-new. There are three types of memory: sensory, short-term, and long-term. Sensory memory is very short, lasting only a couple seconds. Short-term memory lasts a little longer, holding an idea or fact for as long as you think about it. Once your focus changes, the memory will fade in about 20 or 30 seconds. Long-term memory stores large amounts of information. It keeps information on file after you stop thinking about it. Some of this information lasts throughout a person's lifetime. Sometimes short-term memory works with long-term memory, making connections with information already stored in the brain. This is called *working memory.* Making associations in working memory helps make information easier to recall.

Getting Started

Begin the activity by asking your students, "Why do we remember some things but not others?" Have students share their responses with the class. Discuss various mnemonic devices used to help students remember facts (for example, ROY G. BIV for the colors of the rainbow or **n**ever **e**at **s**our **w**atermelon for the directions on a compass). Next, tell the class that they are going to experiment to help determine why they can remember some things but not others. Then guide the class through the steps on page 19 to complete the investigation.

Mnemonic Device

ROY G. BIV = the colors of the rainbow
R = red
O = orange
Y = yellow
G = green
B = blue
I = indigo
V = violet

The Investigation

STEP 1 Direct each student to formulate a hypothesis that answers the question "Why can I remember some things but not others?" and record it on his data collection sheet (page 72).

STEP 2 Spread the items in the supply bag on a table or the floor. Have each student observe the items for two minutes. Cover the objects. Then instruct the student to record as many items as he can remember under List 1 on his data collection sheet. Then have him fold his paper to cover List 1, leaving List 2 exposed.

STEP 3 Explain the importance of association for memory. Tell students that creating a connection between two objects can make them easier to remember. For example, they can link one object to the next by creating a story, a rhyme, or a mental image.

STEP 4 Uncover the objects and have each student observe them again, this time applying the concept of association. After two minutes, cover the items again. Then direct the student to list as many items as possible under List 2 on his sheet.

STEP 5 Have the student complete the results and conclusion sections of his sheet. Allow time for students to share their findings with the class.

Case File Conclusion

Students will most likely be able to recall more items when they created a connection between two bits of information (List 2). If students only repeated items over and over in their heads, they would be using their short-term memory. Short-term memory can hold small amounts of information for short periods of time, so it would be difficult to store 15 items and remember them long enough to write them down.

Further Investigation

If desired, continue this investigation by posing the following questions:
- Does shortening or lengthening the observation time affect the number of items remembered?
- Does decreasing the number of items make remembering them easier?
- Does the type of items displayed affect your ability to recall them?

How Does Bile Help Digest Food?

Help students understand the important role bile plays in the digestion of food with this amazing investigation.

Purpose

To understand bile's role in the digestion of food

Materials

FOR EACH STUDENT
- copy of page 73

FOR EACH GROUP
- clear plastic cup
- ½ c. measuring cup
- water
- 1 tbsp. liquid stain remover
- 1 tbsp. mayonnaise
- plastic spoon

Background for the Teacher

Bile is a thin green liquid that breaks down fats in foods. It is not an enzyme, so it does not actually digest the food. Instead, bile aids digestion by breaking the large fatty pieces into tiny drops that can be digested. Bile is made in the liver and stored in the gall bladder until there is fat to digest. Then it enters the small intestine through the duodenum and begins its work. The body produces up to two pints of bile a day.

Getting Started

Begin the activity by asking your students, "What is bile?" Discuss their responses and then explain that bile helps in the digestion of food. Then tell students that they will complete an experiment that will simulate the effects of bile on food. Divide the students into groups of four. Give each group the materials listed above. Then guide the groups through the steps on page 21 to complete the investigation.

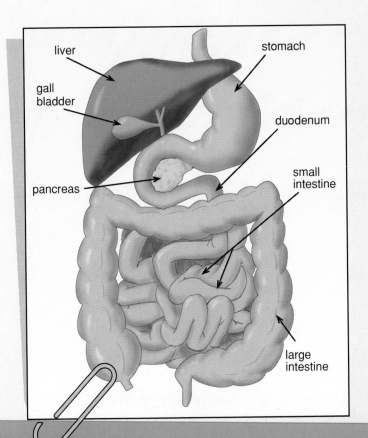

The Investigation

STEP 1 Have each group reflect on the question "How does bile help digest food?" Then instruct each group to formulate a hypothesis that answers the question and have each student record it on the data collection sheet (page 73).

STEP 2 Direct each group to fill its plastic cup with one-half cup of water. Then have the group add one tablespoon of mayonnaise to the water. Have the group observe how the mayonnaise collects on the top of the water. Explain that this simulates fat in the bloodstream.

STEP 3 Next, direct each group to add one tablespoon of liquid stain remover to the cup. Instruct the group to gently stir the stain remover into the water without disturbing the mayonnaise. Explain that the liquid stain remover simulates the bile, which is secreted by the liver.

STEP 4 Have the group observe what happens to the mayonnaise over time. Have group members record their observations at 5, 10, 15, and 20 minutes. Then direct the group members to discuss and complete the results and conclusion sections on their data collection sheets. Set aside time for each group to share its findings with the class.

Case File Conclusion

Most likely the mayonnaise separated, first into smaller chunks, and then to almost a liquid by the end. This process is similar to the action of bile on fats. Once the fats are broken down into smaller particles, they can be more readily absorbed by the body.

Further Investigation

If desired, continue this investigation by posing the following questions:
- Which stain remover brand works most quickly and effectively in breaking down mayonnaise?
- Do other household products work to simulate how bile breaks down fats? Try dishwashing soap, baking soda, soda water, laundry detergent, and shampoo.

How Much Air Can My Lungs Hold?

LIFE SCIENCE CASE NÓ. 9

This investigation provides a breath of fresh air as students investigate their lung capacities!

Purpose

To understand and measure lung vital capacity

Materials

FOR THE TEACHER
- empty 1 L bottle

FOR EACH STUDENT
- large round balloon
- copy of page 74

FOR EACH GROUP
- 1 gal. bucket
- 2 gal. bucket
- large liquid measuring cup with milliliters marked
- access to water

Background for the Teacher

Vital capacity is the amount of air forced out after taking in the deepest breath possible. This measure is comparable to the amount of air that will actually fit in your lungs. The amount of air each person's lungs can hold depends on several factors, including the person's height, gender, and age. A taller person usually has a larger lung capacity than a shorter person. An average male can hold up to six liters of air in his lungs after breathing as deeply as possible. An average female's lungs can store about $4\frac{1}{2}$ liters of air. Lung capacity increases until you are about 20 years old. Then it begins to decrease gradually.

Getting Started

Begin the activity by asking students to take a deep breath in and then exhale. Next, hold up the empty bottle and ask, "If you could measure the amount of air your lungs can hold, how many one-liter bottles would it fill?" Discuss students' responses. Next, tell students that they will be conducting an investigation to measure their lung vital capacities. Divide students into groups of five and distribute the listed materials. Then guide each group through the steps on page 23 to complete the investigation.

The Investigation

STEP 1 Have each student think about the question "How much air can my lungs hold?" Direct him to formulate a hypothesis, using liters as the unit of measure, and record his hypothesis on his data collection sheet (page 74).

STEP 2 Have each student fill in the chart on his data collection sheet with his name, height, and gender, and that of each of his group members. Also, have each student stretch his balloon by blowing it up several times.

STEP 3 Instruct each group to fill its one-gallon bucket with water and place it inside the two-gallon bucket. Have one student from the group use the measuring cup to top off the bucket's water level so that it is exactly level with the rim, making sure not to spill any into the larger bucket.

STEP 4 Have one group member take as deep a breath as possible, blow it out into his balloon, and then tie off the balloon. Explain that once he runs out of air, he cannot take another breath and continue blowing into the balloon. (Caution: Have students stop blowing into the balloon if they begin to feel lightheaded.)

STEP 5 Have the student gently push his inflated balloon into the filled one-gallon bucket, causing some water to be displaced into the two-gallon bucket. Have him carefully remove the one-gallon bucket and then have another student pour the water from the two-gallon bucket into the empty measuring cup. Instruct each group member to record this amount on his data collection sheet and then pour the water back into the one-gallon bucket.

STEP 6 Explain that the amount of water displaced is approximately the same as the amount of air held in the balloon. Have each group repeat Steps 3–5 for each member.

STEP 7 Have each group discuss and complete the results and conclusions sections on their data collection sheets. Set aside time for each group to share its findings with the class.

Case File Conclusion

As each balloon is immersed, the two-gallon bucket holds the water that has been displaced by the balloon. The displaced water is approximately equivalent to the amount of air held in the student's balloon. Students should find that vital capacity varies among the group members.

Further Investigation

If desired, continue this investigation by posing the following questions:
- What happens when you complete this investigation after rigorous exercise?
- Do adults have greater lung capacities than children?
- How can you increase your lung capacity?

How Does Exercise Affect My Heart Rate?

Get your students' pulses pounding with this circulatory system investigation!

Purpose
To examine how exercise and rest affect heart rate

Materials

FOR THE TEACHER
- stopwatch or watch with a second hand

FOR EACH STUDENT
- copy of page 75

Background for the Teacher

The main parts of the circulatory system are the heart, blood, and blood vessels. The heart is a very strong muscle that pumps blood throughout the body using a complicated system of tubes, the blood vessels. The blood brings oxygen and nutrients to the muscles and other parts of the body. The rate at which the heart beats, or pumps blood, automatically adjusts in response to the body's needs. While the body is resting the heart beats slowly. During exercise, muscles need more blood, so the heart pumps faster.

Finding Your Pulse
1. Lay your arm on a table with the palm of your hand up.
2. Place the fingertips of your other hand on your wrist, just below the thumb.
3. Gently press until you can feel your heartbeat. (Note: You may have to move your fingertips around the area until you feel your heartbeat.)

Getting Started

Begin the activity by asking your students, "How does exercise affect your heart rate?" Discuss their ideas. Then tell students that they're going to do an experiment to see how exercise affects heart rate. Explain that each time your heart beats, blood is pumped through your arteries. This can be felt by pressing the skin where an artery is close to the surface. Guide each student through the steps shown to help him practice finding his pulse. Then continue the investigation by guiding each student through the steps on page 25.

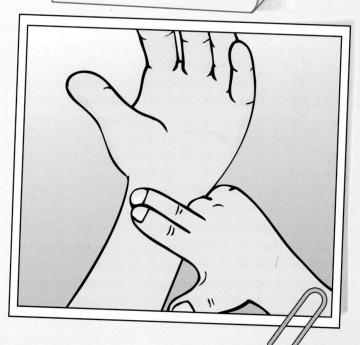

The Investigation

STEP 1 Have each student formulate a hypothesis about which activity listed on the data collection sheet (page 75) will yield the highest heart rate. Then have him record his hypothesis.

STEP 2 Instruct students to sit very still for one minute. Then, on your signal, direct each student to take his pulse for 15 seconds. Have him multiply his pulse by four to get the number of heartbeats per minute and record this rate on his data collection sheet. Instruct students to rest for three minutes. Then guide students in repeating this procedure with each remaining activity, resting for three minutes in between.

STEP 3 Afterward, have each student use his results to complete the bar graph and the results and conclusion sections on his data collection sheet.

Case File Conclusion

Students should observe that their heart rates were slowest during periods of rest (sitting and standing) and fastest during the strenuous exercises (hopping, running in place, doing jumping jacks and sit-ups).

Further Investigation

If desired, continue this investigation by posing the following questions:
- What was the average resting heart rate in the class?
- What other exercises might affect your heart rate?
- Would your results be the same if you did each activity for five minutes?

Which Retains More Water— Sand or Potting Soil?

EARTH SCIENCE CASE NO. 1

Help students soak up knowledge about soil with this earthy investigation!

Purpose
To observe how the texture of a soil affects how much water it can hold

Materials

FOR THE TEACHER
- clean, empty two-liter plastic bottle for each group
- scissors
- ½ c. measuring cup
- ½ c. sand for each group
- ½ c. potting soil for each group
- two coffee filters for each group

FOR EACH GROUP
- copy of page 76
- 2 clear plastic cups
- black crayon
- 2 prepared coffee filters
- prepared funnel
- access to water and paper towels
- liquid measuring cup

Background for the Teacher

A soil's texture affects its ability to retain water. Soils are made up of rock pieces and animal and plant materials. The size of the rock pieces helps determine the soil's texture. Soil with larger rock pieces is considered sand. Soil with smaller rock pieces is considered silt. Soil with the smallest rock pieces is considered clay. Soils made up of larger rock pieces have more space between the pieces, which allows water to drain off quickly. Soils made up of smaller rock pieces have less space between the pieces and retain more water.

Getting Started

In advance, cut the tops from the plastic bottles to make funnels. Next, place half of a cup of sand and half of a cup of potting soil on separate coffee filters for each group. Begin the activity by showing students each type of soil and asking them to describe the characteristics of each. Discuss students' responses and explain that they will conduct an investigation to find out which soil retains more water. Divide students into groups of four and give each group the materials listed above. Guide each group through the steps on page 27 to complete the investigation.

The Investigation

STEP 1 Have each group study its soil samples and reflect on the question "Which retains more water—sand or potting soil?" Direct each group to formulate a hypothesis that answers the question and record it on the data collection sheet (page 76).

STEP 2 Direct each group to use a black crayon to label one clear plastic cup "sand" and the other cup "potting soil." Have students place the bottle funnel in the plastic cup labeled "sand" and put the sand-filled coffee filter in the funnel as shown. Then have them measure one cup of water in the liquid measuring cup. On your signal, direct the group to pour half of a cup of water over the sand in the filter. After 30 seconds, direct the group to pour the other half of a cup of water over the sand. Allow one minute for the water to drain through the sand.

STEP 3 Direct the group to repeat Step 2 using the coffee filter filled with potting soil and the other labeled cup.

STEP 4 Have each group compare the amount of water that drained through the sand with the amount that drained through the potting soil. Next, have the group use the liquid measuring cup to measure the water from each plastic cup. Direct the group to record the data and then complete the results and conclusion sections on the data collection sheet. Set aside time for each group to share its findings with the class.

Case File Conclusion

Because the sand is made up of larger rock pieces than the potting soil, more water should drain through the sand. Potting soil is made up of smaller rock pieces than sand. Students should observe that the water drains through the potting soil more slowly.

Further Investigation

If desired, continue this investigation by posing the following questions:
- Does wet soil hold more water than dry soil?
- Would a mixture of sand and potting soil hold more or less water than potting soil only? Why?

How Does Water Change the Earth's Surface?

Your students will get carried away with this investigation into erosion!

Purpose

To model how the earth's surface changes as a result of erosion by water

Materials

FOR THE TEACHER
- pushpin

FOR EACH STUDENT
- copy of page 77

FOR EACH GROUP
- two 9" aluminum pie pans
- small lump of clay
- 5 small rocks
- ½ c. sand
- ¼ c. topsoil or potting soil
- large plastic cup, prepared as described
- 1 c. water

Background for the Teacher

The earth's surface is constantly attacked by forces that break up and carry away soil and rocks. *Weathering* is the wearing down of rocks by water, wind, and other means. The rock particles created by this process, called sediment, are then carried away due to erosion, often by water. These processes are continuous but are generally slow and can take millions of years to change the earth's surface.

Moving water in rivers, waves, and glaciers is the greatest force changing the earth's surface. These moving waters deposit sediment, creating flood plains along river banks, deltas at the rivers' mouths, and sand on beaches.

Getting Started

In advance, use the pushpin to make five holes in the bottom of each group's plastic cup. Also, use a pencil to make one hole on the inside bottom edge of one pie pan for each group. To begin the investigation, ask students to think about the playground, or other outside area, after a very hard rain. Ask, "How does water change the earth's surface?" Discuss students' responses. Divide students into groups and distribute the materials listed above. Then guide each group through the steps on page 29 to complete the investigation.

The Investigation

STEP 1 Have each group reflect on the question "How does water change the earth's surface?" Direct the group to formulate a hypothesis that answers the question and have each student record it on the data collection sheet (page 77).

STEP 2 Explain to students that they will construct a model of the earth's surface. Have each group layer the half of the pie pan opposite the hole with rocks, sand, and topsoil as shown (Figure 1). Next, instruct each group to mold its clay into a one-inch cube and position it against the inside edge of the other pie pan. Then have each group stack the pans so that the dirt-filled pan rests atop the other pan at an angle, as shown, with the hole at the low end (Figure 2). Explain that the top pie pan represents the earth's surface. Have each student draw this surface on his data collection sheet.

STEP 3 Have one student in each group hold the prepared plastic cup over the uppermost part of the model's surface while another student pours the water into the cup, simulating rain. Instruct students to observe the water and note any changes to the earth's surface. When the cup is empty, have each student draw a second picture of the surface on his data collection sheet and describe the changes he observed both during and after the simulated rain.

STEP 4 Direct the students in each group to discuss and complete the results and conclusion sections on their data collection sheets. Set aside time for each group to share its findings with the class.

Figure 1

Figure 2

Case File Conclusion

The water should flow over the model's surface and seep into the soil and sand. As the water moves, it will likely carry loose particles of soil or sand. The water may also carry away some of the topsoil covering and create gullies in the model surface. The water may deposit sand and soil near the hole in the pie pan to form a small delta. The amount of erosion observed will be affected by the angle of the pan, the soil textures, and the force of the simulated rain.

Further Investigation

If desired, continue this investigation by posing the following questions:
- What happens to the surface when the top pie pan is not angled?
- What happens to the surface when the water cup has larger holes, simulating heavier rains?

How Are Sand and Potting Soil Different?

Help students dig into the differences between potting soil and sand with this hands-on activity!

Purpose

To observe and describe the physical differences between sand and potting soil

Materials

FOR THE TEACHER
- apple
- orange

FOR EACH STUDENT
- a copy of page 78

FOR EACH GROUP
- ½ c. sand
- ½ c. potting soil
- 2 paper plates
- magnifying glass
- small handheld strainer

Background for the Teacher

Each of the three types of rocks—*igneous, metamorphic,* and *sedimentary*—is subject to weathering and erosion. This is part of the *rock cycle,* in which rocks form, break down, and re-form into other types of rocks. When rocks break down, they form soil, which makes up much of the surface of the earth. Sand is one component of soil. Soil also contains other minerals, plant and animal matter, water, and air. Soil can be classified by look, feel, and particle size. There are over 70,000 kinds of soil in the United States.

Getting Started

Begin the investigation by showing students the apple and the orange. Ask students to describe the differences between the fruits. Encourage students to include sensory descriptions of the look, feel, and size of each fruit. After students have practiced comparing and describing the fruits, explain that students will investigate the differences between sand and potting soil. Divide students into groups and distribute the materials listed. Then guide each group through the steps on page 31 to complete the investigation.

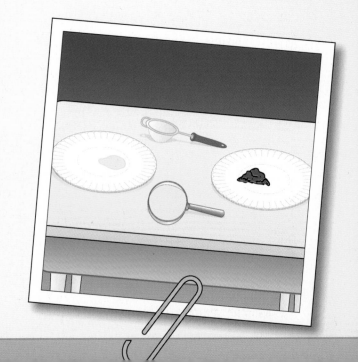

The Investigation

STEP 1 Have each group consider the question "How are sand and potting soil different?" Instruct the group to formulate a hypothesis that answers the question and have each student record it on his data collection sheet (page 78).

STEP 2 Instruct each group to pour the sand and soil each on a separate paper plate. Guide the students to make observations about what each sample looks and feels like, noting the color and texture. Have students in each group take turns using the magnifying glass to examine each sample's components. Direct them to also explore the size of the particles using the strainer. Throughout their examinations, have students record their observations on their data collection sheets.

STEP 3 Direct the group members to discuss and complete the results and conclusion sections on their data collection sheets. Set aside time for each group to share its findings with the class.

Case File Conclusion

Students should observe that sand is lighter in color than soil. Dark soil generally has more partially decomposed plant and animal matter, called humus, than light-colored soil. Individual sand particles may be round or angular and can be seen and felt. Soil has fine particles and should feel like powder. Sand particles are larger than soil particles, so larger grains of sand should remain after the sand has been sifted. After the soil has been sifted, mainly organic materials will remain.

Further Investigation

If desired, continue this investigation by posing the following questions:

- What differences would you observe if both samples were wet?
- Do sand and potting soil have different weights?

How Clean Is the Air at Our School?

Ah-choo! Send your students on a mission to investigate air pollutants at school.

Purpose

To identify possible man-made and natural sources of airborne pollution at school

Materials

FOR EACH GROUP

- copy of page 79
- 2 large index cards
- small cup of petroleum jelly
- magnifying glass
- paper towels
- masking tape
- duct tape

Background for the Teacher

Although some air pollution is caused by nature, man-made air pollution is a more serious problem. Polluted air causes health problems and changes the earth's atmosphere; plus, it erodes monuments and statues. Air pollution occurs as a gas and as particulate matter, which includes tiny particles of things such as dust and soot. Many gases, such as nitrogen and radon, are invisible. But particulate matter is visible when enough of it collects in one place.

Getting Started

Begin the investigation by explaining that millions of tiny particles—some man-made and some naturally occurring—are floating in the air. Tell your students that the air in some locations contains more particulates than the air in other locations. Then ask students, "How clean is the air at our school?" Next, explain to students that they will conduct an investigation to test how clean the air is at different locations in and around the school. Divide the class into groups of four and provide them with the materials listed above. Continue the investigation by guiding each group through the steps on page 33.

Man-Made Pollutants	Natural Pollutants
emissions from furnaces, chimneys, cars, buses, airplanes, and factories smoke from burning garbage	dust pollen soil particles particles and gases from volcanoes

The Investigation

STEP 1 Have each group reflect on the question "How clean is the air at our school?" Direct the group to formulate a hypothesis that answers the question and record it on the data collection sheet (page 79).

STEP 2 Guide each group in selecting one indoor and one outdoor collection site where they will test air quality. (Indoor locations might include the library or the gym. Outdoor locations might include a sheltered area on the playground or the bus-loading area.) Then direct the groups to label the top of each index card with their names and the selected collection site. Next, have each group use a paper towel to spread petroleum jelly in a thin, even layer on the labeled side of each index card.

STEP 3 Instruct each group to visit its first collection site with the cards, tape, and data collection sheet. Have the students secure one of the cards at this site, using masking tape for an indoor location and duct tape for an outdoor location. Have the group observe the surroundings for potential pollutants and record them on its data collection sheet. Then have each group repeat this step with the second index card at the other collection site.

STEP 4 After 24 hours, send each group to collect its cards and then return to the classroom. Provide each group with a magnifying glass with which to observe and count the number and types of *particulates,* or small particles, collected on each card. Have the group record these results and possible sources for the particulates on its data collection sheet.

STEP 5 Have the group complete and then discuss the results and conclusion sections on the data collection sheet. Set aside time for each group to share its findings with the class.

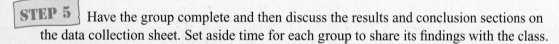

Case File Conclusion

Students should observe a variety of particulates on their cards. Particulates in the air will vary from location to location around the school. There are many different types of activities and materials that contribute to the pollutants in and around the school. For example, the amount of particulate matter may be higher on the playground due to vehicle exhaust, windblown dust, or seasonal pollen.

Further Investigation

If desired, continue this investigation by posing the following questions:

- Will temperature impact the number of particulates collected?
- How might weather affect the number of particulates collected?
- Will varying the height at which the card is placed change the number of particulates collected?

Which Recyclable Material Does Our Class Generate More of in One Week?

Help students understand the positive impact of recycling on the environment with this investigation.

Purpose

To gain understanding of how much recyclable trash one classroom generates weekly

Materials

FOR EACH STUDENT
- copy of page 80

FOR EACH GROUP
- large cardboard box
- colored paper, markers, and other items to decorate the box

---

Background for the Teacher

The average person in the United States throws away four to six pounds of garbage each day. In some places, so much trash is thrown away that landfills are becoming full. One way to reduce trash is by recycling. Recycling involves using the material from an old product to make a new product. Many materials can be recycled, including paper, glass, aluminum, and plastic. Recycling these products helps conserve natural resources and energy. If everyone in North America recycled the Sunday newspaper, more than 500,000 trees per week would be preserved.

Getting Started

Begin the investigation by asking students to explain what it means to recycle. Next, ask the class to name kinds of materials that can be recycled. Write the following recyclables on the board: tin, paper, aluminum, cardboard, glass, and plastic. Ask students to think about which items they use the most and the least. Then explain to students that they will be conducting an experiment to see how much recyclable trash the class creates in one week. Divide the class into six groups and give each group a large cardboard box. Then guide each group through the steps on page 35.

The Investigation

STEP 1 Ask students to reflect c
"Which recyclable material does c
more of in one week?" Direct each s
late a hypothesis that answers the ques
record it on his data collection sheet (pag

STEP 2 Assign each group one of the recycla
listed on the board. Have the group members la
and decorate the outside of their box.

STEP 3 For one full week, have students collect any
of the listed recyclables that would otherwise be
discarded and place them in the appropriate boxes.
(**WARNING:** Remind the group to be careful when
placing glass items into the container.) At the end of
the week, allow time for each group to count the
items in its box and share its data with the class.
Direct each student to fill in the chart on his data
collection sheet.

STEP 4 Have each student use the class data to
create a graph in the space provided on his data collection sheet. Then have the student complete the
results and conclusion sections of his sheet. Allow
time for students to share their findings with the
class.

Case File Conclusion

Since paper is one of the most com-
monly used materials, your students will
likely collect more paper during the week
than any other recyclable.

Further Investigation

If desired, continue this investigation
by posing the following questions:
- How can reusing materials help the
  environment?
- What can we do to reduce the
  amount of trash we create at
  school?

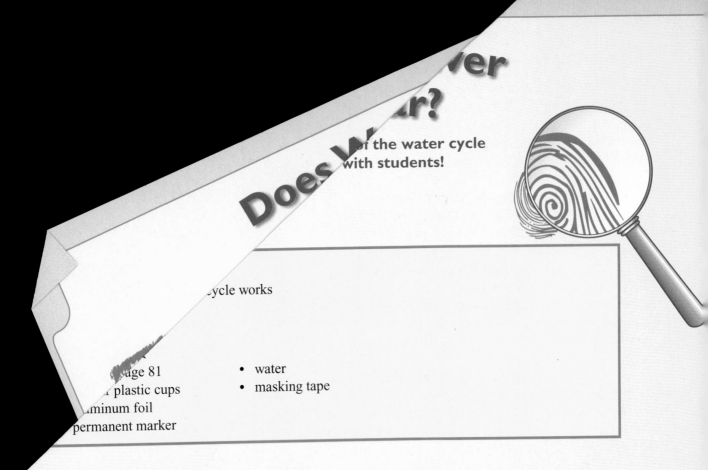

Does W??er?

...of the water cycle
...with students!

...cycle works

...age 81
...plastic cups
...minum foil
...permanent marker

- water
- masking tape

Background for the Teacher

More than 70 percent of the earth is covered with water. The water that is on the earth today is the same water that was on the earth four billion years ago. Water has been cycling since time began. The heat from the sun warms the water from oceans, lakes, and other bodies of water, turning some of it into an invisible gas called water vapor. This process is called evaporation. The water vapor cools as it rises and turns into water droplets (condensation). These droplets form clouds. When enough moisture collects, the droplets fall as precipitation (rain, sleet, hail, or snow). Then the cycle is repeated. Therefore, water never disappears. It changes from a liquid to an invisible vapor and then back to a liquid again.

Getting Started

Begin the investigation by having students think about a puddle of water after a rain shower. Ask students, "Where does this water go?" Lead students to the conclusion that the water evaporates. Then ask, "Does the water disappear when it evaporates?" Take a poll of yes answers and no answers. Next, tell students that they are going to experiment with water to find out the answer themselves. Pair students and give each twosome the supplies listed above. Then guide each pair through the steps on page 37 to complete the investigation.

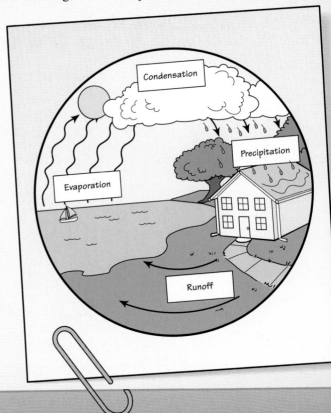

The Investigation

STEP 1 Instruct each pair to discuss what might happen when water evaporates. Does it disappear or does it go somewhere else? Direct each pair to formulate a hypothesis and record it on the data collection sheet (page 81).

STEP 2 Have partners use a permanent marker to label their cups with their initials, and then direct them to fill each cup halfway with water. Have them mark the waterline on each cup with a small piece of masking tape as shown. Next, direct the twosome to securely cover one cup with aluminum foil by pressing the foil firmly against the sides of the cup. Finally, have the pair place its cups in a warm location, such as a windowsill.

STEP 3 Each day for the next three days, allow time for partners to check their cups. Have each pair inspect the outside of each cup, the amount of water inside each cup, and the underside of the foil lid. Instruct the twosome to record its observations each day on the data collection sheet as directed.

STEP 4 After recording the final day's observations, have partners discuss and record their results and conclusion on their data collection sheet. Then invite each pair to share its results with the class.

Case File Conclusion

The amount of water in each cup should decrease. However, the amount of water in the uncovered cup should decrease more since the water vapor is able to escape into the air. The water vapor in the covered cup cannot escape and may collect as tiny water droplets on the underside of the foil lid. Some of these droplets may even fall back into the cup, keeping the water level higher.

Further Investigation

If desired, continue this investigation by posing the following questions:

- Would poking a small hole in the foil lid allow all the water vapor to escape?
- If used as lids, would materials such as paper, plastic, or cloth affect the water level?

How Can You Measure the Wind?

Classroom meteorology will really measure up with this wind investigation.

EARTH SCIENCE CASE NO. 7

Purpose

To construct and use instruments to measure wind direction and wind speed

Materials

FOR THE TEACHER
- yardstick
- compass

FOR EACH GROUP
- copy of page 82
- 7¾" plastic straw
- ruler
- pushpin
- index card
- straight pin
- small bead
- pencil
- small foam cup
- marker
- cotton ball
- 7" length of string
- protractor
- tape
- scissors
- access to a stapler

Background for the Teacher

Wind is air moving across the earth's surface. Wind direction and wind speed are measured to help predict and describe weather. Anemometers can be used to measure wind speed. Weather or wind vanes are used to measure wind direction. Wind is described by the direction from which it blows.

Getting Started

Begin the investigation by holding up the yardstick and asking students what it can measure. Then ask students to name other instruments that are used for measuring. After several examples have been given, ask students what they could use to measure the wind. Guide students to the conclusion that measuring wind requires specific tools or instruments. Divide students into groups and provide them with the listed materials. Then guide each group through the steps on page 39 to complete the investigation.

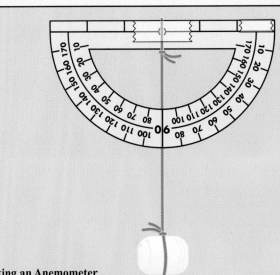

Making an Anemometer
1. Tie one end of the string around the cotton ball.
2. Wrap the other end of the string around the center point of the protractor as shown. Secure it with tape.
3. Place a piece of tape in the corner as indicated. This is the edge that students will point into the wind.
4. To use the anemometer, hold the protractor so that the string hangs straight down at the 90-degree mark.

The Investigation

STEP 1 Have each group reflect on the question "How can you measure the wind?" Direct the group to formulate a hypothesis and to record it on the data collection sheet (page 82).

STEP 2 Guide each group through the directions shown to make a wind vane and an anemometer.

STEP 3 On a windy day, lead each group outside with its wind vane, anemometer, and data collection sheet. Use the compass to identify north so that the groups can aim their wind vanes accordingly. Explain to students that the arrow on the wind vane points in the direction from which the wind is coming. Direct one student in each group to record the wind direction on the group's data collection sheet.

STEP 4 Have a student from each group point the taped corner of the group's anemometer in the direction from which the wind is blowing so that the cotton ball is lifted by the wind. Have another student observe the angle at which the string crosses the protractor, using the numbers on the outside edge. Have the student record the measurement on the group's data collection sheet.

STEP 5 Repeat Steps 3 and 4 at the same outdoor location and time each day for one week.

STEP 6 Direct the group to discuss and complete the results and conclusion sections on the data collection sheet. Set aside time for each group to share its findings with the class.

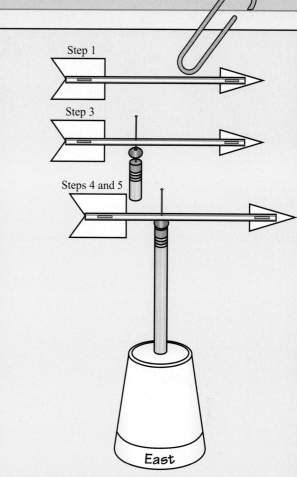

Step 1

Step 3

Steps 4 and 5

East

Making a Wind Vane
1. Cut out a small arrow and a tail from the index card. Staple them to the straw as shown.
2. Use the pushpin to poke a hole in the straw three inches from the tail end.
3. Poke the straight pin through the hole in the straw, through the bead, and then into the pencil's eraser as shown.
4. Label the bottom of the cup with the cardinal directions.
5. Push the pencil through the center of the cup, creating a base as shown.

Case File Conclusion

By establishing north and orienting the wind vane's base accordingly, the wind vane should show the direction from which the wind is coming. With the anemometer, the cotton ball should be lifted by the wind and pull the string along the protractor. The string should cross the protractor at a greater angle as wind speed increases. Students should observe that even with handcrafted instruments, patterns and changes in the wind can be measured and recorded.

Further Investigation

If desired, continue this investigation by posing the following questions:
- How might wind speed and direction change hour by hour?
- How might recording wind speed and wind direction be useful?

Does the Sun Move Across the Sky Each Day?

Use this experiment to shine a little light on the earth's rotation!

Purpose
To understand the sun's position in relation to the earth

Materials

FOR THE TEACHER
- pencil
- Styrofoam brand ball
- small object, such as an eraser or piece of chalk
- small amount of Sticky-Tac
- flashlight

FOR EACH PAIR
- copy of page 83
- pencil
- measuring tape or meterstick
- 3 craft sticks
- marker
- access to a large, grassy area on a sunny day

Background for the Teacher

The earth revolves around the sun. Each revolution takes a little more than 365 days. As the earth revolves around the sun, it also rotates on its axis. Each rotation takes a little less than 24 hours. As the earth rotates it seems that the sun is moving across the sky, rising and setting. What actually happens is one part of the earth is facing the sun, and that part has light. As the earth spins, that side slowly turns away from the sun, and then that part has darkness. As one part of the earth turns away from the sun, another part turns toward it. This cycle repeats itself about every 24 hours.

Getting Started

Begin the activity by asking students, "Does the sun really move across the sky each day?" Take a poll of how many students say yes and how many say no. Have students explain their reasoning. Then ask students if they think their location on the earth affects how they see the sun. Discuss students' responses. Tell students they are going to complete an experiment to further investigate this question. Give pairs of students the supplies listed above. Have them write their initials on one end of each craft stick and then label one stick "Shadow 1" and a second stick "Shadow 2." Guide each pair through the steps on page 41 to complete the investigation.

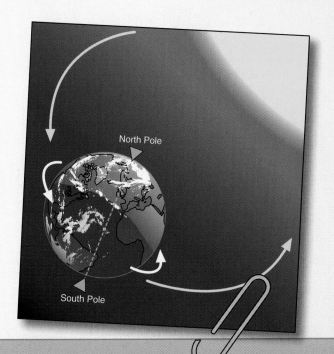

North Pole

South Pole

The Investigation

STEP 1 Have each pair reflect on the question "Does the sun move across the sky each day?" Direct each pair to formulate a hypothesis that answers the question and record it on the data collection sheet (page 83).

STEP 2 Take students to a large, grassy area. Have each pair push the craft stick with just the students' initials on it into the ground. (Make sure the end with the initials is out of the ground.) Have one partner stand beside the stick, facing the direction of his shadow. Direct the other partner to place the craft stick labeled "Shadow 1" at the end of the shadow to mark it. Have the pair measure the distance between the two markers and record the result in the corresponding column on the data collection sheet. Remind pairs to note the time the measurement was taken. Instruct each pair to leave its markers at the site and return to the classroom.

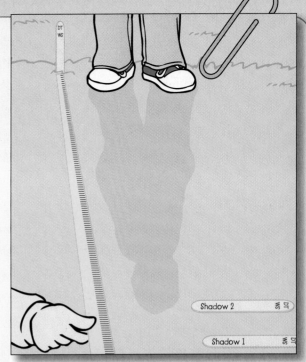

STEP 3 Begin the teacher demonstration by sticking the pencil through the middle of the Styrofoam ball. Explain that the ball represents the earth and the pencil represents the earth's axis. Attach the small object to the ball with the Sticky-Tac to show your approximate location on the earth. Turn off the lights and have a student shine the flashlight on the ball, keeping the light in the same place. Slightly tilt the ball and spin it slowly. Allow time to discuss students' observations and relate them to how the sun appears as the earth rotates on its axis. Remind students that the earth also revolves around the sun.

STEP 4 After one hour, have pairs return to their outdoor experiment spots. Direct each twosome to repeat the process in Step 2, this time using the craft stick labeled "Shadow 2" to mark the end of the shadow. Be sure that students leave the previous marker in place. Also be sure that the same student's shadow is measured. Have pairs measure and record the results on their data collection sheets.

STEP 5 Have students complete the results and conclusion sections on their data collection sheets. Set aside time for each pair to share its findings with the class.

Case File Conclusion

Most likely the shadow lengths changed as the day progressed. This is because the sun's position in the sky changes as the earth rotates on its axis. Shadows are longer when the sun is low and shorter when the sun is high. For example, around noon the sun is almost overhead. This causes shadows to be very short. Whether the sun appears to be low or high depends on the rotation of the earth. It is not because the sun is moving.

Further Investigation

If desired, continue this investigation by posing the following questions:
- Would the results vary if you conducted this investigation at a different time of day?
- Would the results be different during a different season?

Do Stars Move Across the Sky?

This investigation into stars will shed light on how the earth's rotation affects the night sky.

Purpose

To understand that the earth's rotation causes stars to appear to move across the sky

Materials

FOR EACH STUDENT
- copy of page 84

FOR EACH GROUP
- access to a constellation chart
- 3' square of black bulletin board paper
- white chalk

Background for the Teacher

As we look at the night sky, the earth is rotating on its axis. Because the earth is rotating, the stars seem to rotate in the opposite direction. This movement is an optical illusion. As the earth turns, different stars can be seen at different times during the night. Certain groups of stars, or constellations, observed at 8:00 P.M. will appear to have moved when observed a few hours later. Because the earth orbits the sun, different constellations can be seen from different locations on the planet. If the stars were observed each night, they would seem to remain in the same position relative to each other.

Getting Started

Several days prior to the investigation, ask students to observe the night sky for the next few evenings. To begin the investigation, ask, "Do stars move across the sky?" Encourage students to discuss what they saw the previous nights. Then explain to students that they will complete an investigation that will show whether or not the stars move. Divide students into groups of four and distribute the materials listed above. Then guide the groups through the steps on page 43 to complete the investigation.

The Investigation

STEP 1 Guide the students in each group to reflect on the question "Do stars move across the sky?" Direct each group to formulate a hypothesis that answers the question, and have the students record it on their data collection sheets (page 84).

STEP 2 Remind students that a group of stars is called a constellation. Instruct each group to use the chalk to draw four constellations on its bulletin board paper, referring to the constellation chart as a guide.

STEP 3 Direct three students from each group to hold the paper, constellation side down, above their heads. Have the fourth student in each group kneel directly underneath the paper, facing the front of the classroom as Position 1. Explain that the kneeling student is the earth. Instruct this student to look up at the stars on the paper and record what she sees. Remind students that the earth rotates on its axis. Then have the kneeling student slowly rotate to the left, stopping to face each wall and record her observations after each move.

STEP 4 Repeat Step 3 so that each student has an opportunity to act as the earth. Afterward, have the students in each group discuss and complete the results and conclusion sections on their data collection sheets. Set aside time for each group to share its findings with the class.

Case File Conclusion

As each student models the rotation of the earth, the student-drawn constellations should appear to move in the opposite direction.

Further Investigation

If desired, continue this investigation by posing the following questions:
- Can you see the same stars every night?
- Can you see the same stars all year?
- Why can't you see stars during the day?

How Big Are the Planets in Relation to Earth?

This investigation will help your students size up the planets!

EARTH SCIENCE CASE NO. 10

Purpose
To compare the relative sizes of the planets in relation to Earth

Materials
FOR EACH GROUP
- copy of page 85
- calculator
- resealable plastic bag filled with approximately 180 miniature marshmallows
- 6' length of butcher paper
- markers
- glue
- plastic knife

Background for the Teacher

Our solar system is made up of the sun and all the objects that travel around it. The solar system has nine planets: Mercury, Venus, Earth, Mars, Jupiter, Saturn, Uranus, Neptune, and Pluto. The first four planets are called the terrestrial planets. They are mainly made of iron and rock. The next four planets are called the giant planets. They are mainly made of hydrogen, helium, ammonia, and methane. The ninth planet, Pluto, is not classified like the other planets.

Getting Started

Begin the investigation by asking students to share what they know about the solar system. Then ask students, "How big are the planets in relation to Earth?" Discuss students' responses. Tell students that they will complete an activity to investigate the size of each planet. Divide students into groups of four and give each group the materials listed above. Then guide each group through the steps on page 45 to complete the investigation.

Planet	Diameter (in km)
Mercury	4,900
Venus	12,100
Earth	12,756
Mars	6,800
Jupiter	142,800
Saturn	120,660
Uranus	52,400
Neptune	49,500
Pluto	2,300

The Investigation

STEP 1 Have each group reflect on the question "How big are the planets in relation to Earth?" Direct the group to formulate a hypothesis that answers the question and record it on the data collection sheet (page 85).

STEP 2 List on the chalkboard the planets and the diameter of each as shown on page 44. Then have each group record this information on its data collection sheet. Explain that students will use this info to make a scale model of the solar system to investigate the size of each planet, relative to Earth.

STEP 3 Show students a miniature marshmallow. Now ask students, "If one marshmallow equals the diameter of Pluto, how many marshmallows would be needed to represent the diameter of Earth?" Show students that the answer can be found by dividing the diameter of Earth (12,756 km) by the diameter of Pluto (2,300 km) on their calculators. Then explain that the answer is 5½ marshmallows. Have each group write its information on its data collection sheet.

STEP 4 Have students repeat the process to find each planet's diameter, rounding to the nearest half marshmallow. Direct the group to write each planet's marshmallow diameter on its data collection sheet. Then have the group make a scale model to show the size of the planets using the marshmallows, butcher paper, markers, glue, and plastic knife (see Figure 1).

STEP 5 Have each group discuss and complete the results and conclusion sections on its data collection sheet. Set aside time for each group to share its findings with the class.

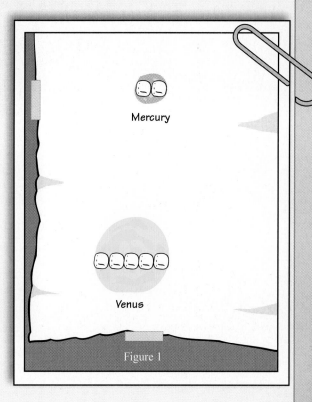

Figure 1

Case File Conclusion

Students should conclude that the planets are all different sizes. The giant planets—Jupiter, Saturn, Uranus, and Neptune—are much larger than Earth. Of the terrestrial planets, Mercury and Mars are much smaller than Earth and Venus is nearly the same size as Earth. Jupiter is the largest planet and Pluto is the smallest.

Further Investigation

If desired, continue this investigation by posing the following questions:
- Does the size of the planet affect how quickly it revolves around the sun?
- Does the size of the planet affect how quickly it rotates on its axis?
- Does the size of a planet affect its number of rings or moons?

Can All States of Matter Be Seen?

Out of sight is out of mind? Not anymore with this fun exploration of air!

Purpose
To determine whether matter can be invisible

Materials

FOR THE TEACHER
- clear jar with lid

FOR EACH GROUP
- 3 balloons
- copy of page 86

Background for the Teacher

Matter can exist in three states: solid, liquid, and gas. A gas has neither a definite shape nor volume. These depend on the size and shape of the container holding the gas. Air is actually a mixture of several gases. Although it is invisible, air can be felt and heard.

Getting Started

Begin the activity by showing students the jar with the lid on it. Ask them what they think is inside the jar. After discussing their responses, explain to your students that they will be experimenting to determine whether all states of matter can be seen. Divide students into groups of three and distribute the materials listed above. Then guide each group through the steps on page 47 to complete the investigation.

Matter
- Anything that has mass and takes up space

- Can exist in three states: solid, liquid, gas.

The Investigation

STEP 1 Instruct each group to reflect on the question "Can all states of matter be seen?" Direct the group to formulate a hypothesis that answers the question and record it on the data collection sheet (page 86).

STEP 2 Have one student from each group blow up one balloon and seal the opening by pinching it. Instruct the student holding the balloon to slightly release the pressure and listen. Then have him record what he heard.

STEP 3 Have a different student from each group blow up a second balloon and pinch the opening shut. Instruct the student to securely hold his balloon as he places the opening of his balloon near a group member's hand and then releases the air. Have the group member record what he felt.

STEP 4 Finally, have the third student in each group blow up the remaining balloon and pinch the opening shut. Direct her to release the balloon and observe what happens. Have the student record her observations. Then have the group discuss and complete the results and conclusion sections on its data collection sheet. Set aside time for each group to share its findings with the class.

Case File Conclusion

Students should observe that although the gas in the balloons cannot be seen, its presence is evident because the balloons are inflated. Students' breath (a gas) fills the balloons and takes the balloons' shape. Students should have heard the air escaping from the openings of the balloons, felt it blowing on their hands, and seen it propel the balloons around the room.

Further Investigation

If desired, continue this investigation by posing the following questions:
- What would happen if your teacher put a jar over a burning candle?
- What would happen if you put a jar upside down into a bucket of water?

Can Water Exist in All Three States of Matter?

Help students understand water's properties with this investigation.

Purpose
To discover a common material that exists in all three states of matter

Materials

FOR EACH PAIR
- copy of page 87
- 3 oz. Dixie cup
- water

FOR THE TEACHER
- glass stovetop pot
- hot plate (WARNING: To be operated by the teacher only)

Background for the Teacher

Matter makes up all things. Matter comes in three states: *solid, liquid,* and *gas.* Matter cannot be created nor destroyed, but it can change form depending upon temperature. If a solid is heated, it can melt and become a liquid. If the liquid continues to be heated, the molecules then escape the surface, or *evaporate,* and become a gas. The rate of evaporation depends upon the intensity of the heat. In the same manner, cooling matter can also change its state. Cold temperatures can cause liquids to freeze into solids. While other substances can exist in all three states of matter, water is unusual because it exists in all three states under normal temperatures.

Getting Started

In advance, make arrangements with school cafeteria workers to have access to a freezer. Begin the investigation by asking students to name and describe the three states of matter. Then ask students, "Can water exist in all three states of matter?" Discuss students' answers. Tell students that they're going to experiment to test their answers. Divide students into pairs. Next, give each pair the materials listed above. Then guide the pairs through the steps on page 49 to complete the investigation.

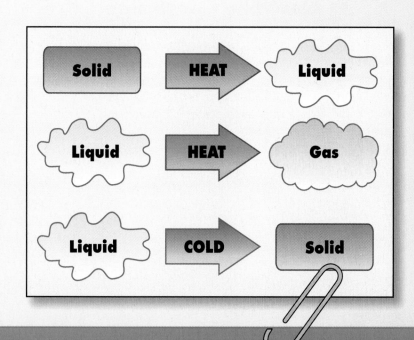

The Investigation

STEP 1 Have students reflect on the question "Can water exist in all three states of matter?" Direct each pair to formulate a hypothesis that answers the question and record it on the data collection sheet (page 87).

STEP 2 Have each pair fill its Dixie cup half full with water. Instruct the pair to identify the water's state of matter and record it on the data collection sheet. Next, have the pair place the cup in the freezer. Then wait at least two hours before continuing the investigation.

STEP 3 After waiting, have each pair remove its cup from the freezer. Instruct the pair to examine the cup and again record the water's state of matter on the data collection sheet.

STEP 4 Direct each pair to remove the ice from its cup by peeling the paper from around it. Have each pair place its ice in the cooking pot. Then place the pot on the hot plate and heat the ice until it begins to melt. From a safe distance, have students observe the steam that rises from the pot, recording the water's state of matter on their data collection sheets. If desired, allow the water to heat until it all has turned to water vapor and none is left in the pot. Remove the pot from the hot plate as soon as all the water has evaporated to prevent the pot from scorching. Immediately turn off the hot plate and put it and the pot in a safe place to cool.

STEP 5 Direct each pair to complete the results and conclusion sections on the data collection sheet. Allow time for class discussion.

Case File Conclusion

Students should observe that the water in the cup is in liquid form, the frozen water is in solid form, and the steam is in gas form. Point out that as the water becomes a gas, eventually it also becomes invisible.

Further Investigation

If desired, continue this investigation by posing the following questions:
- What would happen if your teacher held a pie tin or sheet of metal over heated water?
- Besides temperature, does anything else cause matter to change?

Is Kool-Aid Drink a Mixture or a Compound?

Compound your students' interest in chemistry with this experiment!

Purpose
To understand the difference between mixtures and compounds

Materials

FOR THE TEACHER
- saucepan
- hot plate (**WARNING:** To be operated by the teacher only)

FOR EACH GROUP
- copy of page 88
- resealable plastic bag
- coffee filter
- 3 tbsp. water
- plastic cup
- ½ tsp. Kool-Aid powdered drink mix
- measuring spoons

Background for the Teacher

Mixtures are formed when different substances are combined and the original substances can be separated from each other. For a compound to form, two or more substances combine chemically so that the original parts can't be separated by physical means, such as filtering, sifting, or heating.

Getting Started

To begin the investigation, ask your students to define mixtures and compounds in their own words. Discuss student responses and define the terms. Then ask students whether they think Kool-Aid drink is a mixture that can be separated back into water and the powdered mix or a compound that is a completely new substance and can't be separated. Divide students into groups of four. Then guide each group through the steps on page 51 to complete the investigation.

Figure 1

The Investigation

STEP 1 Have each group reflect on the question "Is Kool-Aid drink a mixture or a compound?" Direct the group to formulate a hypothesis that answers the question and record it on the data collection sheet (page 88).

STEP 2 Have each group pour three tablespoons of water into the resealable plastic bag and record its observations about the water on the data collection sheet. Then have the students add ½ teaspoon of Kool-Aid powdered drink mix. Direct one student to seal the bag and then mix the ingredients by gently squeezing the bottom of the bag. Have the group record its observations.

STEP 3 Have one member of each group fold the coffee filter into quarters as shown in Figure 1 and open it over the mouth of the plastic cup. Direct another student to carefully pour the mixed Kool-Aid drink and water through the filter. Have the group record its observations on the data collection sheet.

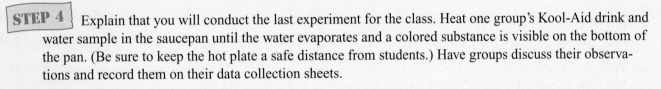

STEP 4 Explain that you will conduct the last experiment for the class. Heat one group's Kool-Aid drink and water sample in the saucepan until the water evaporates and a colored substance is visible on the bottom of the pan. (Be sure to keep the hot plate a safe distance from students.) Have groups discuss their observations and record them on their data collection sheets.

STEP 5 Direct each group to discuss and complete the results and conclusion sections on its data collection sheet. Set aside time for each group to share its findings with the class.

Case File Conclusion

Kool-Aid drink is a mixture because the original substances can be separated. When the Kool-Aid powder and water were heated, the water evaporated and the Kool-Aid powder was left in the bottom of the saucepan. The two substances did not combine chemically.

Further Investigation

If desired, continue this investigation by posing the following questions:

- If Kool-Aid powder were mixed with a different liquid, would the results of the experiment be different?
- Besides heating, in what ways might mixtures and solutions be separated?

How Does Heat Affect Matter?

PHYSICAL SCIENCE CASE NO. 4

This energetic investigation will help students understand how heat affects matter!

Purpose

To observe and describe how matter changes when it is heated

Materials

FOR THE TEACHER
- 3 tennis balls
- clear tennis ball container with label removed

FOR EACH GROUP
- copy of page 89
- snack-size resealable plastic bag containing 1tbsp. chocolate chips
- foam cup
- access to a clock
- access to hot and cold water
- 2 clear plastic cups
- food coloring
- balloon
- clean, empty clear plastic bottle (16 oz.)
- measuring cup
- plastic container (slightly larger than the bottle)

Background for the Teacher

Matter is made up of molecules, which are always moving. In a solid, molecules are close together and only vibrate in place. In a liquid, molecules are spread out and move around more and move more quickly. In a gas, molecules are far apart and move around a lot and very quickly. When matter is heated, the molecules move faster. As molecule movement increases, the matter may change to a different state but it is still the same matter. For example, water can be heated to make steam or ice can be melted to make water, but all of these are still forms of water.

Getting Started

Write the words *solid, liquid,* and *gas* on the board. Ask students to share what they already know about these states of matter. Explain that the molecules in all states of matter are constantly moving. Demonstrate this concept by shaking the tennis ball container back and forth with all three balls inside. Explain that the molecules in a solid are close together and do not move very much. Remove one ball and repeat, explaining that the molecules in liquids are not as close together and move back and forth more freely. Then remove another ball and repeat, explaining that the molecules in gases are further apart and move rapidly to fill the available space. Next, ask students, "How does heat affect matter?" After allowing students to share their thoughts, divide them into groups and distribute the listed materials. Guide the groups through the steps on page 53 to complete the investigation.

The Investigation

STEP 1   Have students reflect on the question "How does heat affect matter?" Direct each group to formulate a hypothesis that answers the question and record it on the data collection sheet (page 89).

STEP 2   Instruct each group to fill the foam cup halfway with hot tap water. Have the group place its bag of chocolate chips inside the cup and observe what happens for three minutes. Direct the group to record its observations on the data collection sheet and then pour out the water.

STEP 3   Next, direct each group to fill one plastic cup with cold water and the other with warm water. Have the group add one drop of food coloring to each cup and observe what happens for three minutes. Then instruct the group to record its observations.

STEP 4   Have each group place the neck of the balloon over the water bottle's opening. Next, have one student in the group pour one cup of hot water into the plastic container and then set the bottle inside. Have the group observe the balloon for one minute and record its observations.

STEP 5   After cleaning up, direct each group to discuss and complete the results and conclusion sections on the data collection sheet. Set aside time for each group to share its findings with the class.

Case File Conclusion

Students should observe that when the chocolate chips are heated, they soften. The food coloring will likely spread out faster in the warm water than the cold because the molecules in the warm water are moving faster. As the air in the water bottle heats up, the molecules will likely move faster, causing the balloon to begin to inflate.

Further Investigation

If desired, continue this investigation by posing the following questions:
- What properties of the chocolate chips did not change when you heated them? Why?
- What would happen to the balloon if the hot water were replaced with ice water?

Which Conducts Sound Better: Air or a Solid?

With this investigation into sound, hearing is believing!

Purpose
To observe whether air or a solid material is a better conductor of sound

Materials

FOR EACH PAIR

- 2 copies of page 90
- pencil
- plastic ruler
- wooden spoon
- metal spoon
- small bottle of water

Background for the Teacher

Sound is caused by an object's vibrations. The vibrations pass from one molecule to another in waves. Sound waves move away from vibrating objects and travel at different speeds, depending on the material through which they travel. Sound waves travel the fastest through solids because the molecules are close together and can be quickly transferred from one molecule to another. With gases, such as those in the air, the molecules are farther apart, so the sound waves are not transferred as quickly. When a human ear picks up sound waves, they are translated into nerve impulses. These impulses travel to the brain where the sound is interpreted.

Getting Started

Begin the activity by reviewing with students the fact that sound travels in waves. Next, ask your students, "Which conducts sound better: air or a solid?" Discuss students' responses. Divide students into pairs and give each pair the materials listed above. Explain to students that they will compare sounds heard in the air with sounds heard through a desktop. Then guide each pair through the steps on page 55 to complete the investigation.

The Investigation

STEP 1 Have each pair reflect on the question "Which conducts sound better: air or a solid?" Direct the pair to formulate a hypothesis that answers the question and direct each student to record it on her data collection sheet (page 90).

STEP 2 Direct one partner to lay her head down with her ear against the desktop. Have her use her hand to cover the other ear; then ask her to listen carefully. Have the other student place the plastic ruler on the desk one foot away and lightly tap the ruler with the pencil.

STEP 3 Have the student lift her head from the desk and listen as her partner taps the ruler again. Direct the listener to rate the loudness of each sound on her data collection sheet.

STEP 4 Instruct each pair to switch roles and repeat Steps 2 and 3. Then have them repeat the entire process by tapping the pencil on each material listed on the data collection sheet.

STEP 5 Have students in each pair discuss and complete the results and conclusion sections on their data collection sheets. Set aside time for each pair to share its findings with the class.

Case File Conclusion

Students will probably agree that regardless of which object they are using, they can hear the sound better through the desk. They will most likely conclude that sound travels better through a solid than through the air.

Further Investigation

If desired, continue this investigation by posing the following questions:

- What happens when the objects are placed closer to the person listening?
- What happens when you listen through a water balloon instead of a desk?
- Do the results differ when you place a cloth between the desk and each object?

Can Light Bend?

Seeing is believing for your young scientists with this awesome investigation of light!

Purpose
To observe how light bends as it passes through an object

Materials
FOR EACH GROUP
- copy of page 91
- 9" x 12" sheet of black construction paper
- 9" x 12" sheet of white construction paper
- scissors
- clear plastic cup
- water
- flashlight
- tape
- ruler

Background for the Teacher
   Light is an energy form that travels freely through space. When there is nothing to delay its travel, light moves at a speed of 186,282 miles per second. Light travels at different speeds through different objects. When it passes from one transparent material to another, it changes direction, or bends. This change in direction is called *refraction*.

Getting Started
   Begin the activity by asking your students if they have ever looked at a straw in a glass of water or observed their feet at the bottom of a swimming pool. Invite students to explain what they've observed in these situations. Then tell your students that they're going to experiment with light to find out what causes these occurrences. Divide students into groups of three. Guide each group through the steps on page 57 to complete the investigation.

The Investigation

STEP 1 Direct students to reflect on the question "Can light bend?" Have each group formulate a hypothesis that answers the question and record it on the data collection sheet (page 91).

STEP 2 Next, direct each group to fold its black paper in half to 9" x 6". Instruct the group to tape the paper's edges and then cut a ⅛" x 4" slit starting at the center of the folded edge.

STEP 3 Have the group lay the white paper horizontally on a table. Show one group member how to hold the black paper vertically along the top edge of the white paper. Then have a second group member shine the flashlight from behind the black paper and through the slit onto the white paper as shown. Instruct the third group member to trace the lighted path on the white paper and label it "air." Direct a group member to record on the data collection sheet whether the light was bent or not bent.

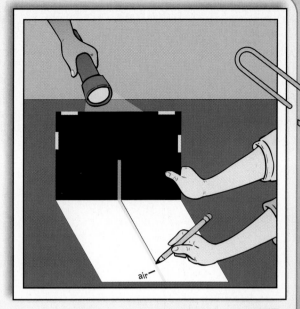

STEP 4 Direct the group to fill its cup with water. Have the group place the cup on the white paper about six inches in front of where the slit will be. With one student holding the black paper and one student holding the light, have the third student trace the path created when the light beam passes through the cup of water, labeling it "water." Direct a group member to record the results on the data collection sheet.

STEP 5 Have each group study its test results. Then direct the group to discuss and complete the results and conclusion sections on the data collection sheet. Allow time for each group to share its findings with the class.

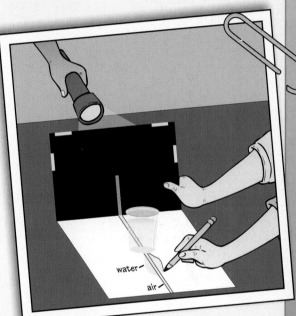

Case File Conclusion

Most likely students saw a straight path of light shine through the paper slit when no medium was blocking its path. When the cup of water was placed in the path of the light, the speed of the light slowed down, causing the light path to bend, or refract.

Further Investigation

If desired, continue this investigation by posing the following questions:
- Does the light's angle affect refraction?
- Do items other than clear plastic refract light?
- Do liquids other than water refract light?

What Happens When an Object Is Pulled in Opposite Directions?

Pull a few strings for better understanding of force and motion with this quick investigation!

Purpose
To observe the effects of opposite forces acting on an object

Materials

FOR THE TEACHER
- ⅝" inch or larger metal washer for each pair
- two 1' lengths of twine for each pair

FOR EACH PAIR
- copy of page 92
- prepared metal washer
- 2" strip of masking tape

Background for the Teacher

A force is a push or a pull that makes something start moving, stop moving, or change direction. If an object is not moving, a push or a pull will set it in motion. If an object is moving, a push or a pull will change its speed or direction. If a moving object receives a push in the same direction, it will move faster. If an object moving in a straight line is pushed from the side, it will change direction. Multiple forces acting on an object are called *concurrent forces*. If the concurrent forces are balanced, the object will not move. If one force is stronger than the other, the object will move in the direction of the stronger force.

Getting Started

In advance, prepare a metal washer for each pair by following the directions shown. Then begin the investigation by pointing to an object, such as a chair, and asking your students how it can move. Discuss students' responses. Next, review with students that an object cannot move itself. Explain that a force, such as a push or pull, will make an object move. Then ask students, "What happens when an object is pulled in opposite directions?" Tell students that they will complete a series of tasks to investigate their predictions. Divide students into pairs and distribute the materials listed. Then guide each pair through the steps on page 59 to complete the investigation.

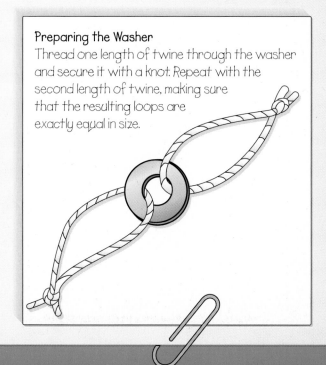

Preparing the Washer
Thread one length of twine through the washer and secure it with a knot. Repeat with the second length of twine, making sure that the resulting loops are exactly equal in size.

The Investigation

STEP 1 Have each pair reflect on the question "What happens when an object is pulled in opposite directions?" Direct the pair to formulate a hypothesis that answers the question and record it on the data collection sheet (page 92).

STEP 2 Direct each pair to position the tape strip horizontally in the center of a desktop. Then have the students center the washer over the tape strip, with the loops extending perpendicular from it. Instruct partners to stand on opposite sides of the desk, each with a loop facing him.

STEP 3 Direct the pairs to complete each task listed and record their observations on the data collection sheets. Explain to students that they must keep the washer flat on the desk for each task.

STEP 4 Have each pair discuss the investigation and complete the results and conclusion sections on the data collection sheet. Set aside time for each pair to share its findings with the class.

Case File Conclusion

Students should observe that the washer will not move in task 1 because no force is acting on it. In task 2, there is one force acting on the washer, so it should move away from the tape strip. Because tasks 3–5 involve concurrent forces, the movement of the washer will depend on the equivalency of the forces being applied. When both loops are pulled with equal force, the washer should not move. When one student pulls or holds with more strength than the other, the washer should move in the direction of the stronger force.

Further Investigation

If desired, continue this investigation by posing the following questions:
- What would happen if you tied a third loop to the washer and all three were pulled with equal force?
- What would happen if the two loops were pulled with equal force from the same side of the washer?

What Makes a Paper Airplane Fly Farther?

Take to the skies with this fun investigation of flight and watch in awe as your young aviators perform breathtaking science-investigation maneuvers.

Purpose

To observe how various modifications can affect the flight of paper airplanes

Materials

FOR EACH STUDENT
- 9" x 12" sheet of construction paper
- copy of page 93
- clipboard or other sturdy writing surface
- pen or pencil
- yardstick

FOR THE CLASS
- supply bag: plastic zippered bag containing various items such as tape, glue, scissors, feathers, pennies, and paper clips
- tape measure
- masking tape

Background for the Teacher

Stability is very important in paper airplane flying. There are three types of stability to keep in mind—*pitch stability, directional stability,* and *roll stability.* In order for a plane to have good pitch stability, more weight is needed toward the front of the plane. Directional stability keeps the plane flying straight. Having fins on the back of the wings helps increase this type of stability. Roll stability keeps the wings level, which helps keep the plane from circling or plummeting to the ground in a spiral. To ensure roll stability, make sure the wings and body together form a Y-shape.

Getting Started

Begin the activity by asking your students, "What makes a paper airplane fly farther?" List their responses on the board and discuss how each listed item might affect the flight. Then tell your students that they're going to experiment with paper airplanes to test their answers. Then give each student the materials listed above. Next, guide each student through the steps shown in Figure 1 for making a paper airplane out of the 9" x 12" sheet of construction paper. Continue the investigation by guiding each student through the steps on page 61.

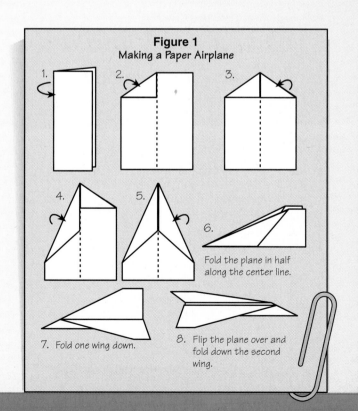

Figure 1
Making a Paper Airplane

1.
2.
3.
4.
5.
6. Fold the plane in half along the center line.
7. Fold one wing down.
8. Flip the plane over and fold down the second wing.

The Investigation

STEP 1   Have each student bring her paper airplane and the class materials to a large, open area (inside or outside). Share with students the items in the supply bag. Then have them reflect on the question "What makes a paper airplane fly farther?" Direct each student to formulate a hypothesis that answers the question and record it on her data collection sheet (page 93).

STEP 2   Use tape to make a start line. Have each student, in turn, stand behind the start line and throw her plane. After the throw, have the student measure and record on the data collection sheet the flight distance as well as a brief description of the flight.

STEP 3   Next, direct student to use the items in the class supply bag to modify her plane to support her hypothesis. Have each student complete a second throw and then measure and record the results on her data collection sheet.

STEP 4   Return to the classroom and have students study their results. Then direct each student to complete the results and conclusion sections on her data collection sheet. Set aside time for each student to share her findings with the class.

Case File Conclusion

Most likely the planes that flew farthest were planes containing more pitch stability and directional stability. (Due to the particular paper airplane used, each plane contained roll stability because of the Y-shaped design of the wings.) Stability kept the planes flying smoothly forward. The strength and control of the throw would also have had an effect on the distance of the flights. Other factors unrelated to the student modifications and throws, such as wind conditions, could also have affected the flight distances.

Further Investigation

If desired, continue this investigation by posing the following questions:
- Would a different kind of paper make the plane fly better?
- Would decreasing or increasing the size of the sheet of paper make the plane fly farther?
- Does a fast or slow throw make the plane fly farther?

Why Do the Lights Go Out When You Flip the Switch?

PHYSICAL SCIENCE CASE NO. 9

Switch on your students' interest in electrical circuits with this electrifying investigation!

Purpose

To understand that electrical circuits require a complete path through which a current can pass

Materials

FOR EACH GROUP

- size C battery
- two 9" strips of aluminum foil
- clear tape
- copy of page 94

- large metal paper clip
- flashlight bulb
- scissors
- ruler

Background for the Teacher

Electricity is energy formed by the flow of electrons. Electricity can occur naturally or it can be man-made. Electric current is the flow of electrons in a conductor through a closed circuit. For an electrical circuit to work, there has to be a complete path from the source of power (like a battery), through the energy receiver (like a lightbulb), and back to the source. A switch is the device that opens or closes the circuit.

Getting Started

To begin the demonstration, ask a student to turn off the classroom lights. Challenge students to describe why the lights went off when the switch was flipped. Discuss students' responses. Then explain to students that they are going to build models to test their answers. Divide students into groups of four and then distribute the listed materials. Guide each group through the steps on page 63 to complete the investigation.

The Investigation

STEP 1 Instruct each group to examine its materials and reflect on the question "Why do the lights go out when you flip the switch?" Direct each group to formulate a hypothesis that answers the question and record it on the data collection sheet (page 94).

STEP 2 Have the group place the battery with its flat end down on one end of one foil strip. Next, have students wrap one end of the other foil strip around the metal part of the lightbulb, securing it with tape. (Be sure the small metal tip on the bottom of the bulb is not covered.) Then have them tape the other end of the foil strip to the top of the battery. (See Figure 1.)

STEP 3 Direct the group to touch the metal part of the bulb to the foil strip that is beneath the battery and record what happens on the data collection sheet.

STEP 4 Have each group remove the foil strip that is beneath the battery and cut a one-inch section from the center. Then have them replace the foil as shown and record what happens. (See Figure 2.) Next, have the group place the paper clip between the cut strips of foil and record what happens. (See Figure 3.)

STEP 5 Direct the group to discuss and complete the results and conclusion sections on the data collection sheet. Set aside time for each group to share its findings with the class.

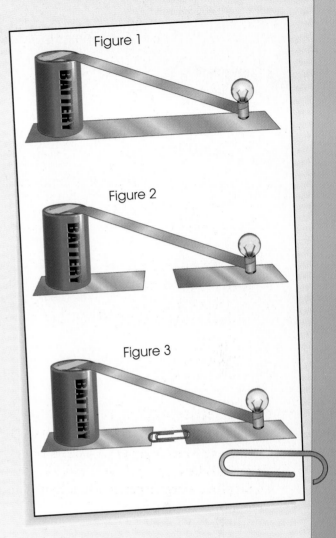

Figure 1

Figure 2

Figure 3

Case File Conclusion

Students should observe that the bulb lights up when the foil strip is uncut. This is because the circuit is complete, allowing electricity to flow. The bulb should not light up when the foil is cut because the flow of electricity is interrupted. When the paper clip is used to connect the sections of the cut foil, the bulb should light up again. The paper clip acts as a switch that closes the circuit.

Further Investigation

If desired, continue this investigation by posing the following questions:
- What other objects could be used in place of the paper clip?
- What do you think happens when there are two switches on one circuit?

What Makes an Object a Good Conductor of Electricity?

PHYSICAL SCIENCE CASE NO. 10

Add some spark to your study of conductors and electricity with this hands-on investigation!

Purpose
To identify the characteristics of good conductors

Materials

FOR THE TEACHER
- wire cutters
- strand of miniature holiday lights
- supply of thin insulated copper wire

FOR EACH GROUP
- copy of page 95
- 9-volt battery
- 2 prepared sections of copper wire
- masking tape
- prepared lightbulb
- quarter
- plastic lid
- penny

- rubber band
- nail
- piece of cloth
- brass paper fastener
- paper clip
- eraser
- ⅛ c. water mixed with ½ tsp. salt

Background for the Teacher

A conductor is a material that allows electricity to flow through it easily. Good conductors have electrons or ions that flow freely through the material. When electricity is applied, these charged particles spread over the material's surface. Metals, living trees, animals, and liquid cleaners are all good conductors. An insulator does not allow electricity to pass through it easily. The atoms of an insulator have such a tight hold on their electrons that few, if any, flow through the material. Good insulators include plastic, glass, rubber, and dry wood.

Getting Started

In advance, use wire cutters to cut a strand of miniature holiday lights into single-bulb sections (one for each group). Then strip one-half inch of plastic from each end of each section as shown. Also, cut the copper wire into eight-inch sections (two for each group) and strip one inch of plastic from each end.

To begin the investigation, remind students that a circuit is a complete path in which an electrical current flows. Review the definitions of electrical conductors and insulators and then ask students, "What makes an object a good conductor of electricity?" After discussing students' responses, explain that they are going to construct a simple circuit to explore the characteristics of good conductors. Divide students into groups and distribute the listed materials. Guide each group through the steps on page 65 to complete the investigation.

The Investigation

STEP 1 Have each group reflect on the question "What makes an object a good conductor of electricity?" Direct each group to formulate a hypothesis that answers the question and record it on the data collection sheet (page 95).

STEP 2 Guide each group through the steps shown to make a simple circuit tester.

STEP 3 Have the group touch the wires' loose ends to the quarter and record whether or not the object conducted the electricity and made the lightbulb light up. Instruct the group to continue in this manner, testing each object from the list.

STEP 4 Direct the group to discuss and complete the results and conclusion sections on the data collection sheet. Set aside time for each group to share its findings with the class.

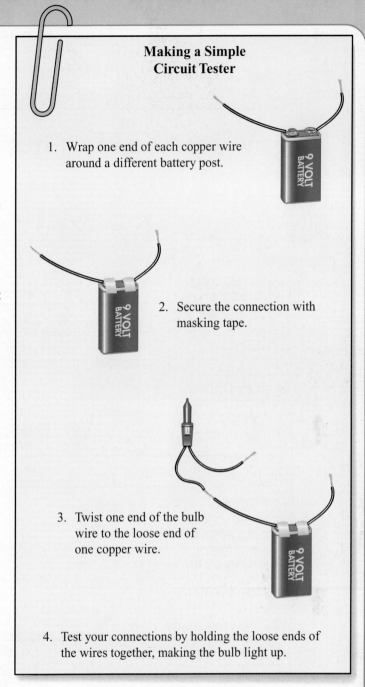

Making a Simple Circuit Tester

1. Wrap one end of each copper wire around a different battery post.

2. Secure the connection with masking tape.

3. Twist one end of the bulb wire to the loose end of one copper wire.

4. Test your connections by holding the loose ends of the wires together, making the bulb light up.

Case File Conclusion

Students should have observed that the quarter, penny, nail, brass paper fastener, paper clip, and saltwater were all good conductors. They likely completed the circuit, causing the bulb to light up. Students should have observed that the plastic lid, rubber band, cloth, and eraser were all insulators. They likely did not complete the circuit and did not cause the bulb to light up.

Further Investigation

If desired, continue this investigation by posing the following questions:
- Are there any metals that are not good conductors of electricity?
- Does a material's shape affect its conductivity?

Why Are My Thumbs Important?

Name _____

Hypothesis
_____

_____

_____

Testing Data

Task	With Thumbs		Without Thumbs	
	Easy	Difficult	Easy	Difficult
opening/closing a zipper				
unwrapping candy				
turning pages in a book				
shuffling cards				
picking up a dime				
writing your name				

Results
Which tasks were easier to perform? Which tasks were more difficult? Explain. _____

_____

_____

Conclusion
Was your hypothesis correct or incorrect?_____
Explain why you think this is so. _____

_____

_____

_____

How Can a Polar Bear Survive in the Arctic?

LIFE SCIENCE CASE NO. 2

Names _____

Hypothesis _____

_____

_____

Testing Data

Group Member	Hand in Shortening-Covered Glove	Hand in Plain Gloves
1		
2		

Results Which hand felt colder? _____

What effect did the Crisco shortening have on the temperature? _____

_____

Conclusion Was your hypothesis correct or incorrect?_____

Explain why you think this is so. _____

_____

_____

_____

If a Penguin Has Wings, Why Can't It Fly?

Names _____

Hypothesis _____

_____

_____

Testing Data

Wing Size	Time Needed to Reach Floor
4 inches	
2 inches	
1 inch	
$\frac{1}{2}$ inch	

Results Which wing size took the longest time to reach the floor? _____

The shortest time? _____ Explain why you think this happened. _____

_____

_____

_____

Conclusion Was your hypothesis correct or incorrect?_____

Explain why you think this is so. _____

_____

_____

_____

How Can Living Things Be Classified?

LIFE SCIENCE CASE NO. 4

Names _____

Hypothesis _____

_____

Testing Data

_____ Name Description: _____ _____ _____	_____ Name Description: _____ _____ _____
_____ Name Description: _____ _____ _____	_____ Name Description: _____ _____ _____

Results Were you able to sort all your beans into different groups? _____

Why or why not? _____

_____

Conclusion Was your hypothesis correct or incorrect? _____

Explain why you think this is so. _____

_____

_____

How Do Flowers and Bees Work Together?

Name_____

Hypothesis _____

_____

_____

Testing Data

Cup	Original Color of Fruit Drink Powder (Pollen)	Colors of Pollen After "Gathering Nectar"
A		
B		
C		

Results What did you observe on each flower and cotton swab at the end

of the experiment? _____

_____

Conclusion Was your hypothesis correct or incorrect?_____

Explain why you think this is so. _____

_____

Explain why you think a bee needs a flower and a flower needs a bee. ____

_____

_____

_____

What Is Inside a Plant Cell?

Name _____

| **Hypothesis** | _____ |

_____

_____

| **Testing Data** |

| **onion skin cell** |

_____   ( )   _____

_____   _____

| **Results** | Which cell parts did you see? _____

_____

Which cell parts were hard to find? _____

_____

| **Conclusion** | Was your hypothesis correct or incorrect? _____

Explain why you think this is so. _____

_____

_____

Why Can I Remember Some Things but Not Others?

LIFE SCIENCE CASE NO. 7

Name _____

Hypothesis _____

_____

_____

Testing Data

List 1

1. _____ 6. _____ 11. _____
2. _____ 7. _____ 12. _____
3. _____ 8. _____ 13. _____
4. _____ 9. _____ 14. _____
5. _____ 10. _____ 15. _____

List 2

1. _____ 6. _____ 11. _____
2. _____ 7. _____ 12. _____
3. _____ 8. _____ 13. _____
4. _____ 9. _____ 14. _____
5. _____ 10. _____ 15. _____

Results Which list is longer? _____ Why? _____

_____

Conclusion Was your hypothesis correct or incorrect?_____

Explain why you think this is so. _____

_____

_____

_____

_____

How Does Bile Help Digest Food?

LIFE SCIENCE CASE NO. 8

Name _____

Hypothesis _____

_____

_____

Testing Data

Time	Description of Cup Contents
0 minutes	
5 minutes	
10 minutes	
15 minutes	
20 minutes	

Results

Draw a picture of the cup at 0 minutes.

Draw a picture of the cup at 20 minutes.

What happened to the mayonnaise in the cup?

_____

_____

_____

0 minutes   20 minutes

Conclusion Was your hypothesis correct or incorrect?_____

Explain why you think this is so. _____

_____

_____

_____

How Much Air Can My Lungs Hold?

Name _____

Hypothesis (Use liters as your unit of measure.)

_____

_____

Testing Data

Name	Height	Gender	Water Displaced (mL/L)

Results Who had the highest vital capacity in your group? _____

Who had the lowest? _____

Why do you think this is so? _____

_____

_____

Conclusion Was your hypothesis correct or incorrect? _____

Explain why you think this is so. _____

_____

_____

_____

How Does Exercise Affect My Heart Rate?

Name _____

Hypothesis For which activity do you think your heart rate will be

highest? _____ Lowest? _____

Explain your hypothesis. _____

_____

Testing Data

1. Record your heart rate.

    Sitting _____ Standing _____ Hopping _____ Running in place _____

    Doing jumping jacks _____ Doing sit-ups _____

2. Graph your heart rate.

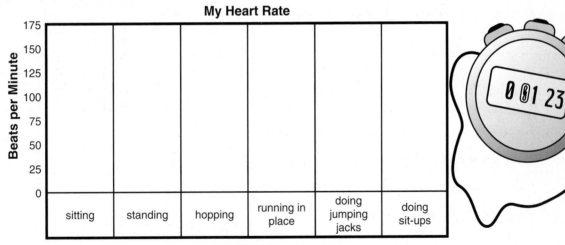

Results For which activity was your heart rate highest? _____

Lowest? _____

Conclusion Was your hypothesis correct or incorrect? _____

Explain why you think this is so. _____

_____

_____

Which Retains More Water— Sand or Potting Soil?

Names _____

Hypothesis _____

_____

_____

Testing Data

Amount of water poured in

Type of soil

Amount of water drained out

Results | Did sand or potting soil hold more water? _____

_____

Conclusion | Was your hypothesis correct or incorrect? _____

Explain why you think this is so. _____

_____

_____

_____

_____

_____

How Does Water Change the Earth's Surface?

EARTH SCIENCE CASE NO. 2

Name _____

Hypothesis _____

_____

_____

Testing Data

Earth surface model
before rain

During the rain, I observed that

_____

_____

_____

_____

_____

Earth surface model
after rain

After the rain, I observed that _____

_____

_____

Results   In what way did the water change the surface of your model?

_____

_____

Conclusion   Was your hypothesis correct or incorrect?_____

Explain why you think this is so. _____

_____

_____

How Are Sand and Potting Soil Different?

Name _____

Hypothesis _____

_____

_____

Testing Data

	Sand	Potting Soil
What I see		
What I feel		
When we sifted		

Results Based on your observations, write a brief description of sand and a brief description of potting soil.

Sand _____	Potting Soil _____
_____	_____
_____	_____
_____	_____

Conclusion Was your hypothesis correct or incorrect?_____

Explain why you think this is so. _____

_____

_____

How Clean Is the Air at Our School?

EARTH SCIENCE CASE NO. 4

Names _____

Hypothesis _____

_____

_____

Testing Data

Location	Potential Sources of Pollution	Number of Particulates	Type of Particulates	Possible Sources of Particulates

Results Which site had more particulates? _____

Why do you think this is so? _____

_____

Conclusion Was your hypothesis correct or incorrect?_____

Explain why you think this is so. _____

_____

_____

_____

Which Recyclable Material Does Our Class Generate More of in One Week?

Name _____

Hypothesis _____

_____

_____

Testing Data

Recyclable Material	Number of Pieces
Tin	
Paper	
Aluminum	
Cardboard	
Glass	
Plastic	

How Much We Recycled in One Week

Number of Pieces

tin   paper   aluminum   cardboard   glass   plastic

Recyclable Material

Results | Which recyclable material was collected the most? _____

The least? _____

Conclusion | Was your hypothesis correct or incorrect?_____

Explain why you think this is so. _____

_____

_____

_____

Does Water Ever Disappear?

Names _____

Hypothesis _____

_____

_____

Testing Data

Draw a line on each cup to show the approximate water level.

Day 1	Day 2	Day 3
Observations:	Observations:	Observations:

Results What happened to the water level in the uncovered cup? _____

_____

What happened to the water level in the covered cup? _____

_____

Conclusion Was your hypothesis correct or incorrect?_____

Explain why you think this is so. _____

_____

_____

How Can You Measure the Wind?

Names _____

Hypothesis _____

_____

_____

Testing Data

	Day 1	Day 2	Day 3	Day 4	Day 5
wind direction					
wind speed					

Results How did the wind vane measure the wind? _____

_____

_____

How did the anemometer measure the wind? _____

_____

_____

Conclusion Was your hypothesis correct or incorrect? _____

Explain why you think this is so. _____

_____

_____

Does the Sun Move Across the Sky Each Day?

EARTH SCIENCE CASE NO. 8

Names _____

Hypothesis _____

_____

_____

Testing Data

Shadow	Time Measurement Was Taken	Length of Shadow (centimeters)
1		
2		

Results Which shadow was the longest? _____

The shortest? _____

Explain why you think this happened. _____

_____

_____

_____

Conclusion Was your hypothesis correct or incorrect?_____

Explain why you think this is so. _____

_____

_____

_____

Do Stars Move Across the Sky?

Name _____

Hypothesis _____

_____

_____

Testing Data

	What I Saw
Position 1	
Position 2	
Position 3	
Position 4	

Results | What did you notice as you rotated? _____

_____

_____

_____

Conclusion | Was your hypothesis correct or incorrect?_____

Explain why you think this is so. _____

_____

_____

How Big Are the Planets in Relation to Earth?

Names _____

Hypothesis _____

_____

_____

Testing Data

Planet	Diameter in Kilometers	Diameter in Mini Marshmallows
Mercury		
Venus		
Earth		
Mars		
Jupiter		
Saturn		
Uranus		
Neptune		
Pluto		

Results Which planet is the largest? _____

The smallest? _____

Explain how you know this is so. _____

_____

Conclusion Was your hypothesis correct or incorrect?_____

Explain why you think this is so. _____

_____

_____

Can All States of Matter Be Seen?

Names _____

Hypothesis _____

_____

_____

Testing Data

Action	Effect
Slightly release the pressure and listen.	
Release the air on a group member's hand.	
Release the full balloon.	

Results

I heard _____

I felt _____

I saw _____

Conclusion Was your hypothesis correct or incorrect?_____

Explain why you think this is so. _____

_____

_____

_____

Can Water Exist in All Three States of Matter?

PHYSICAL SCIENCE CASE NO. 2

Names _____

Hypothesis _____

_____

_____

Testing Data

Water	State		
in cup	☐ solid	☐ liquid	☐ gas
after freezing	☐ solid	☐ liquid	☐ gas
after heating	☐ solid	☐ liquid	☐ gas

Results Based on the data above, describe the changes in matter that you observed. _____

_____

What caused the changes? _____

_____

Conclusion Was your hypothesis correct or incorrect? _____
Explain why you think this is so. _____

_____

_____

_____

Is Kool-Aid Drink a Mixture or a Compound?

PHYSICAL SCIENCE CASE NO. 3

Names _____

Hypothesis _____

_____

_____

Testing Data

Substance	Observations
Water	
Water mixed with Kool-Aid powder	
Water and Kool-Aid powder after filtering	
Water and Kool-Aid powder after heating	

Results   Is Kool-Aid drink a compound or a mixture? How can you tell?

_____

_____

Conclusion   Was your hypothesis correct or incorrect?_____

Explain why you think this is so. _____

_____

_____

_____

_____

How Does Heat Affect Matter?

Names _____

Hypothesis _____

_____

_____

Testing Data

Material	State of Matter	Changes Observed
chocolate chips		
food coloring		
air		

Results How did heat affect the matter in each material? _____

_____

_____

Conclusion Was your hypothesis correct or incorrect? _____

Explain why you think this is so. _____

_____

_____

_____

Which Conducts Sound Better: Air or a Solid?

Name _____

Hypothesis _____

_____

_____

Testing Data

Mark an X on the line to show the loudness of each sound.

Object	Sound Through Solid	Sound Through Air
plastic ruler	quiet ├─┼─┼─┼─┼─┤ loud	quiet ├─┼─┼─┼─┼─┤ loud
wooden spoon	quiet ├─┼─┼─┼─┼─┤ loud	quiet ├─┼─┼─┼─┼─┤ loud
metal spoon	quiet ├─┼─┼─┼─┼─┤ loud	quiet ├─┼─┼─┼─┼─┤ loud
small bottle of water	quiet ├─┼─┼─┼─┼─┤ loud	quiet ├─┼─┼─┼─┼─┤ loud

Results When could you hear the sounds better? _____

_____

Conclusion Was your hypothesis correct or incorrect?_____

Explain why you think this is so. _____

_____

_____

_____

Can Light Bend?

PHYSICAL SCIENCE
CASE NO. 6

Names ____

Hypothesis ____

____

____

Testing Data

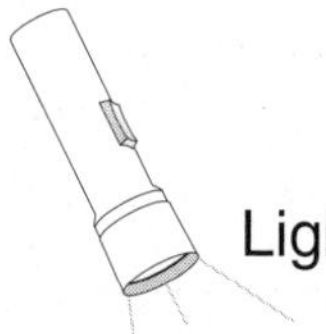

Light beam without interference   bent ☐   not bent ☐

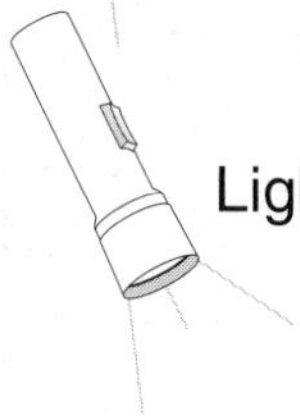

Light beam with interference   bent ☐   not bent ☐

Results How did shining the light through the water-filled cup change the path of the beam? ____

____

____

____

Conclusion Was your hypothesis correct or incorrect?________________

Explain why you think this is so. ____

____

____

____

What Happens When an Object Is Pulled in Opposite Directions?

Names _____

| Hypothesis | _____ |

_____

_____

Testing Data

Task	Force	Movement
1. No one pulls either loop.	☐ none ☐ one ☐ more than one	☐ no movement ☐ movement occurs
2. One student pulls a loop.	☐ none ☐ one ☐ more than one	☐ no movement ☐ movement occurs
3. Each student pulls the loop equally hard.	☐ none ☐ one ☐ more than one	☐ no movement ☐ movement occurs
4. One student pulls harder than the other.	☐ none ☐ one ☐ more than one	☐ no movement ☐ movement occurs
5. One student pulls both loops in opposite directions.	☐ none ☐ one ☐ more than one	☐ no movement ☐ movement occurs

Results What relationships did you notice between the washer's

movements and the forces that were applied to it? _____

_____

Conclusion Was your hypothesis correct or incorrect?_____

Explain why you think this is so. _____

_____

_____

What Makes a Paper Airplane Fly Farther?

PHYSICAL SCIENCE CASE NO. 8

Name _____

Hypothesis _____

_____

_____

Testing Data

	Modification	Flight Distance	Flight Description
Throw 1	None		
Throw 2			

Results Which plane produced the longest flight? _____

_____

Conclusion Was your hypothesis correct or incorrect? _____

Explain why you think this is so. _____

_____

_____

_____

_____

Why Do the Lights Go Out When You Flip the Switch?

Names _____

Hypothesis	_____

_____

_____

Testing Data

	What happens?
BATTERY	
BATTERY	What happens?
BATTERY	What happens?

Results | Which item acts as a switch? _____

How? _____

_____

Conclusion | Was your hypothesis correct or incorrect?_____

Explain why you think this is so. _____

_____

_____

What Makes an Object a Good Conductor of Electricity?

PHYSICAL SCIENCE CASE NO. 10

Names _____

Hypothesis _____

_____

_____

Testing Data

Object	Object's Characteristics
1. quarter	
2. plastic lid	
3. penny	
4. rubber band	
5. nail	
6. piece of cloth	
7. brass fastener	
8. paper clip	
9. eraser	
10. saltwater	

Conductor

Insulator

Results   Which objects conducted electricity? _____

_____

What characteristics do the conductors have in common? _____

_____

Conclusion   Was your hypothesis correct or incorrect?_____

Explain why you think this is so. _____

_____

_____

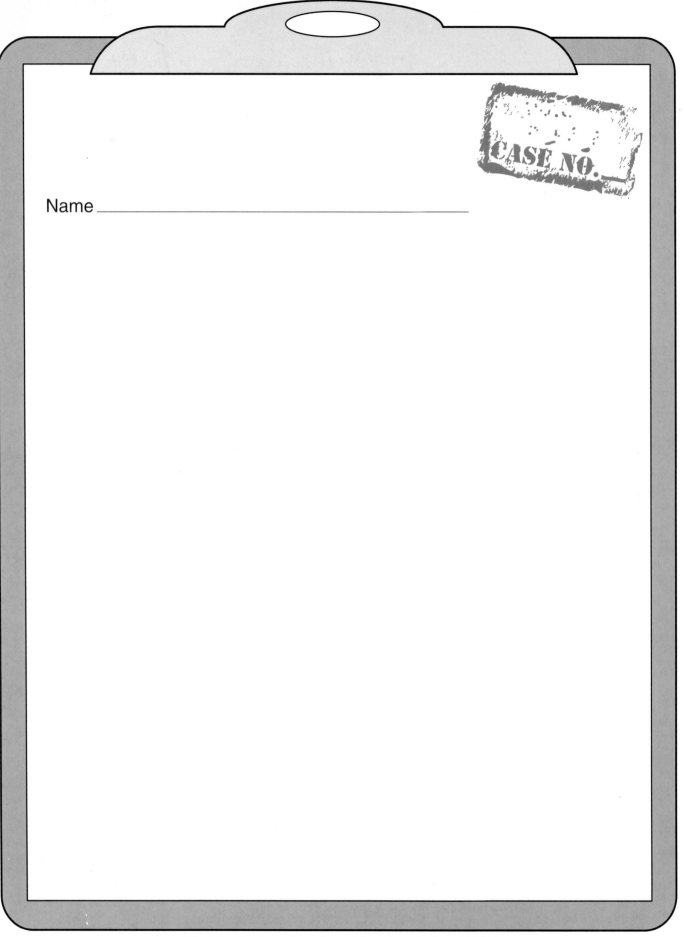

CASE NO.

Name _____